Chrisp's

TRUE CRIME

MISCELLANY

Chrisp's
TRUE CRIME
MISCELLANY

STORIES • FACTS • TALES & TRIVIA

BY PETER CHRISP
WITH T. G. FIELDWALKER

METRO BOOKS
NEW YORK

METRO BOOKS
New York

An Imprint of Sterling Publishing
387 Park Avenue South
New York, NY 10016

METRO BOOKS and the distinctive Metro Books logo are
trademarks of Sterling Publishing Co., Inc.

This book was conceived, designed, and produced by Ilex Press

ILEX PRESS
210 High Street, Lewes, East Sussex, BN7 2NS, UK
PUBLISHER Alastair Campbell
CREATIVE DIRECTOR James Hollywell
MANAGING EDITOR Nick Jones
SENIOR EDITOR Ellie Wilson
COMMISSIONING EDITOR Tim Pilcher
ART DIRECTOR Julie Weir
DESIGNER Lisa McCormick
PICTURE RESEARCHER Katie Greenwood

ISBN 978-1-4351-5701-9

For information about custom editions, special sales, and premium and corporate
purchases, please contact Sterling Special Sales at 800-805-5489 or
specialsales@sterlingpublishing.com.

Manufactured in China

2 4 6 8 10 9 7 5 3 1

www.sterlingpublishing.com

"No man in the wrong can stand up to a man
in the right who just a keeps on a coming."

MOTTO OF THE TEXAS RANGERS

THE GREAT GOLD ROBBERY

THE MOST CLEVERLY PLANNED CRIME of the 19th century was the Great Gold Robbery of May 15, 1855. It was the work of a professional thief called Edward Agar. He learned from William Pierce, a former railway employee, that the London to Folkestone train regularly carried gold bullion, to be shipped to Paris. In 1854, Agar recruited William George Tester—a railway clerk, who supplied him with a wax impression of one of the two keys to the safe—and James Burgess, a railway guard.

To get the second key he needed, Agar sent his own shipment, of £200 in gold to Folkestone. When he went to collect it, he saw where the clerk kept the key. He then watched the office until the clerk briefly left, when he hurriedly made a wax impression of the key.

Agar waited to rob the train until Burgess told him that it would be carrying a particularly large shipment of £14,000 in gold sovereigns. Dressed as gentlemen, Agar and Pierce bought first class tickets at London Bridge Station, and boarded the train, carrying bags loaded with lead weights. Helped by Burgess, Agar opened the safe, and emptied the boxes of gold sovereigns, replacing an equal weight of lead. It was only when the boxes were opened in Paris, that the theft was finally discovered.

In August 1855, Agar was arrested for passing a forged cheque. In prison, he learned that Pierce had betrayed him, by keeping Agar's share of the gold. He then confessed to the gold robbery.

Edward Agar died in a penal colony in Australia. Towards the end of his life, a newly arrived convict told him he had become a legend among the London criminal underworld. Agar replied, "That means nothing, nothing at all!" The heist was made into a book and film, *The First Great Train Robbery*, written and directed by Michael Crichton, and starring Sean Connery as Pierce and Donald Sutherland as Agar.

—— ELIZABETHAN CRIMINAL SLANG ——

THE EARLIEST GLOSSARIES OF CRIMINAL slang date from the Elizabethan age. Many relate to swindling and begging—then a crime punishable with a whipping.

ABRAM-MAN: a beggar who feigns madness

ANGLER: a thief who uses a pole fitted with a hook, to steal from windows; also called a curber and a hooker

BEAK: a magistrate

BUDGE A BEAK: flee from the law

BUNG: a purse

CLY THE JERK: to be whipped

CONY: a dupe or victim (the word means a tame rabbit)

CONY-CATCHING: theft through trickery

COUNTERFEIT CRANK: a beggar who feigns epilepsy

CUTTLE-BUNG: cutpurse's knife

DIVER: a thief who uses a small boy to wriggle into rooms through narrow spaces

DOMMERAR: a beggar who feigns dumbness

FIGGING LAW: cutpurse's art

FULLAMS: weighted dice

FOISTER: a pickpocket

LIFT: to rob a shop or private room

MARKER: accomplice of one who steals from shops

MORT: a woman

NIPPER: a cutpurse; "nipping a bung" means stealing a purse

PRIGGER OF PRANCERS: a horse thief

QUEER KEN: prison

SETTER: first of a group of tricksters to strike acquaintance with the prospective victim

SHAVE: to steal a small article, such as a spoon

TRINING CHEATS: gallows

UPRIGHT MAN: leader of a gang of beggars

WARP: a lookout man

JOACHIM KROLL (1933-1991)

GERMAN SERIAL KILLER AND CANNIBAL, Kroll, AKA "The Ruhr Cannibal" and "The Duisburg Man-Eater" was convicted of eight murders, but confessed to a total of 14 between 1955 and 1976. Kroll only killed in the same place on a few occasions, but years apart. This, and the unnerving fact that there were a number of other serial killers also operating in the area at the time, helped him to elude capture. Kroll would surprise his victims and strangle them quickly. He was arrested on July 3, 1976 for kidnapping and killing a four-year old girl, Marion Ketter. He was charged with eight murders and one attempted murder and given nine life sentences. He died of a heart attack in Rheinbach Prison in 1991.

'NDRANGHETA

CALABRIA, THE TOE OF ITALY, is the homeland of "'Ndrangheta." Though less well known than the Sicilian Mafia or Neapolitan Camorra, the 'Ndrangheta is bigger than either. It has around 10,000 members worldwide, with branches in the USA, Canada, Australia, Germany, France, the Netherlands, Argentina, and Columbia.

'Ndrangheta, pronounced "en-drang-ay-ta," is a Calabrian dialect word, from the Ancient Greek *andragathos*, meaning a "courageous man." Calabrians also use a verb, *'ndranghitiari*, meaning, "to show bravery and defiance."

Although founded in the 19th century, the organization first attracted media attention in the late 1970s, when it began to kidnap wealthy northern Italian businessmen, keeping them in remote Calabrian caves until their families had paid a ransom.

'Ndrangheta is notorious for its violent internal disputes. From 1985–1991, a bloody war between two 'Ndrangheta factions in the city of Reggio Calabria cost more than 700 lives.

In the 1990s, 'Ndrangheta moved into the international drugs trade, importing cocaine from Columbia. Today, it is estimated that 80% of the cocaine entering Europe arrives from Columbia through the Calabrian port of Gioia Tauro.

Unlike the Mafia or Camorra, 'Ndrangheta clans are held together by real ties of blood. Clans, called 'ndrine, are extended families, linked by marriage with other clans. In 2006, Nicola Gratteri, an Italian prosecutor, said, "'Ndrangheta families have often arranged weddings to solder the links between them. There are families that have intermarried as many as four times in the 20th century." As a result, it is almost impossible to get members to become informers. According to Gratteri, "A Calabrian mobster considering turning state's evidence has to come to terms with betraying maybe 200 of his relatives."

ACRONYMS: A

A/O: Often used in case reporting, abbreviation for Arresting Officer.
ABH: Actual Bodily Harm.
ADW: Assault with a Deadly Weapon.
ATF: Bureau of Alcohol, Tobacco, Firearms and Explosives. An American Federal department.

MOHOCKS

IN EARLY 1712, THE STREETS of London were terrorized by a group of upper-class young men who called themselves Mohocks, after the American Mohawk tribe. According to *The Spectator* of March 1712, "The President is styled Emperor of the Mohocks and his Arms are a Turkish Crescent, which his Imperial Majesty bears at present in a very extraordinary manner engraven on his forehead."

The Mohocks would get drunk, and then take to the streets, attacking watchmen and members of the public, whose faces they would cut. The poet and playwright John Gay wrote a farce about them, in which he said that they put women in barrels and rolled them down the street:

> *Who has not trembled at the Mohock's name?*
> *Was there a watchman took his hourly rounds*
> *Safe from their blows, or new-invented wounds?*
> *I pass their desperate deeds and mischiefs, done*
> *Where from Snowhill black steepy torrents run;*
> *How matrons, hooped within the hogshead's womb,*
> *Were tumbled furious thence; the rolling tomb.*
> *O'er the stones thunders, bounds from side to side.*

NED KELLY ON THE POLICE

IN FEBRUARY 1879, THE AUSTRALIAN BUSHRANGER Ned Kelly robbed the bank of Jerilderie in New South Wales. Before leaving town, Kelly handed a 7,379 word letter to the local newspaper, explaining, "I want to say a few words about why I'm an outlaw." This is how he described the police in his letter:

> "*Is my brothers and sisters and my mother not to be pitied also*
> *who has no alternative only to put up with the brutal and cowardly*
> *behavior of a parcel of big, ugly, fat-necked, wombat-headed, big-bellied,*
> *magpie-legged, narrow-hipped, splay-footed sons of Irish bailiffs or English*
> *landlords, which is better known as officers of Justice, or Victorian Police,*
> *who some calls honest gentlemen. But I would like to know what business*
> *an honest man would have in the Police, as it is an old saying, It takes*
> *a rogue to catch a rogue . . . A Policeman is a disgrace to his country,*
> *not alone to the mother that suckled him. In the first place he is*
> *a rogue in his heart, but too cowardly to follow it up without*
> *having the Force to disguise it.*"

PIERREPOINT THE HANGMAN

ALBERT PIERREPOINT WAS A BRITISH public hangman, who executed at least 400 people between 1944 and 1956. In his memoirs, *Executioner: Pierrepoint* (1974), he described his attitude to the death penalty, "I have come to the conclusion that executions solve nothing, and are only an antiquated relic of a primitive desire for revenge, which takes the easy way and hands over the responsibility for revenge to other people. I have seen prison officers faint on the scaffold, strong men weep, and women officers sobbing helplessly. I have known prison doctors who could not examine the body after execution, because the beat of their own heart was obliterating anything they could distinguish."

18TH CENTURY PRISON

18TH CENTURY PRISONS were not designed to punish or reform criminals. They were places to hold them while they awaited trial or punishment. In prison, men, women, and children mixed freely together, and debtors mixed with murderers and lunatics. In *The State of Prisons*, 1775, John Howard, the penal reformer, wrote, "In some Gaols you may see (and who can see it without pain?) boys of 12 or 14 eagerly listening to the stories told by practiced and experienced criminals, of their adventures, successes, stratagems, and escapes."

The keepers, who were unpaid, lived by extorting money from the prisoners, who had to pay for food, drink, straw for bedding, and even fresh air. Every prisoner was fitted with leg irons and other fetters, which were removed for a fee for "easement of irons."

The greatest danger was gaol fever (typhus) spread by lice. It was estimated that each year a quarter of English prisoners died from typhus, which also spread from prisons to the free population. There was a particularly bad outbreak in 1750, when an epidemic, which began in Newgate Prison, struck the Court of the Old Bailey. Among the dead were lawyers, jurymen, the Under Sheriff, and the Lord Mayor. As a result, the prison, and all the prisoners, were sterilized by being washed down with vinegar.

—— TONI MANCINI (1908-1976) ——

MANCINI HAD MOVED TO BRIGHTON, England, with his girlfriend Violette Kaye in 1933. Their tempestuous relationship ended with the petty criminal beating the former dancer and prostitute to death with a hammer. He hid her body in a trunk in his lodgings at 52 Kemp Street, using it as a table. Police discovered the body and Mancini panicked and went on the run, being arrested in South East London. He was found not guilty by a jury but confessed to the murder in an interview with the *News of the World* newspaper just before his death. This was the second "Brighton Trunk Murder" in 1934, and, although both were unrelated, it led to the seaside resort of Brighton being dubbed, "The Queen of Slaughtering Places."

—————————— ACRONYMS: B ——————————

BFT: Blunt Force Trauma. Trauma caused to a body part, either by impact, injury, or physical attack.

—————— THE COUNTERFEIT ROCKEFELLER ——————

POSSIBLY ONE OF THE MOST successful modern day con men was Christophe Thierry Rocancourt (AKA Christopher Rocancourt). The Frenchman allegedly pulled his first scam in Paris, faking the deed to a property he didn't own, then "selling" the property for an impressive $1.4 million. Buoyed by this success he moved to America, convincing a whole slew of wealthy and famous "marks" that he was a French member of the Rockefeller family, and getting them to invest millions of dollars in a variety of schemes. He operated at least a dozen aliases, making out that Sophia Loren was his auntie and his "uncles" were fashion designer Oscar de la Renta and producer Dino De Laurentiis. In L.A. he pretended to be an ex-boxer and movie producer, shared a house with Mickey Rourke, managed to convince Jean-Claude Van Damme to produce his next movie, and married *Playboy* model Pia Reyes.

He was busted in 1998 for being involved in a shootout. He jumped bail and was arrested again in 2000 in the Hamptons for not paying his hotel bill. He escaped over the border, but on April 27, 2001, he, and the unsuspecting Reyes, were arrested in Canada, and extradited to the USA in 2002. In New York he pleaded to charges of theft, grand larceny, smuggling, bribery, perjury, and fraud against 19 victims. He was fined $9 million, ordered to pay $1.2 million in restitution, and sentenced to five years in prison. The Swiss police connected him with a jewel theft and barred him from the country until 2016.

In 2006 he estimated on NBC's Dateline that he had netted approximately $40 million. He has written several books on his exploits and remains unrepentant, "I would not consider myself as a criminal. I steal with my mind. If I take things, if that is your definition of a criminal, then I am a criminal."

"Society wants to believe it can identify evil people, or bad or harmful people, but it's not practical. There are no stereotypes."
TED BUNDY (1946–1989) *US serial killer*

> *"The larger crimes are apt to be the simpler, for the bigger the crime,*
> *the more obvious, as a rule, is the motive."*
>
> SIR ARTHUR CONAN DOYLE (1859–1930)
> *The Adventures of Sherlock Holmes*

INKY DABS

WHILE FINGERPRINTING, also known as dactyloscopy, had been used as far back as 206BCE in China, it wasn't until 1788, that German anatomist Johann Christoph Andreas Mayer confirmed that fingerprints are unique to each individual. Almost a century later, in 1880, Scottish surgeon Dr. Henry Faulds published a paper in the scientific journal *Nature*, suggesting fingerprints for identification, and proposed recording them with ink. He established their first classification and was the first to identify fingerprints left on a vial. In 1886, he offered the concept to the Metropolitan Police in London, but the idea was dismissed. Charles Darwin's cousin, Francis Galton, then spent a decade studying fingerprints, and encouraged their use in forensic science in his book *Finger Prints*. He'd estimated that the chance of a "false positive" (two individuals having the same fingerprints) was about 1 in 64 billion.

A Fingerprint Bureau was established in Calcutta, India, in 1897, which formed the basis of Sir Edward Richard Henry's classification system, which was eventually adopted by Scotland Yard, London, in 1901. In the United States, Dr. Henry P.

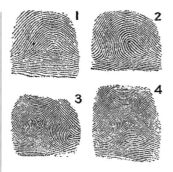

DeForrest used fingerprinting in the New York Civil Service in 1902, and by 1906, fingerprint advocate New York City Police Department Deputy Commissioner Joseph A. Faurot introduced the fingerprinting of criminals to America.

The first case to be solved, and lead to the arrest and conviction of a murderer, based solely upon fingerprint evidence, was in France in 1902. A thief, Henri-Léon Scheffer, had killed a dentist's assistant and had left his dabs on a broken glass case. Scheffer had previously been arrested and his prints were on file. The police officer, and inventor of the mug shot, Alphonse Bertillon made the connection.

—— THE KILLING OF GEORGE CORNELL ——

O N MARCH 9, 1966, THE EAST END gangster Ronnie Kray shot George Cornell in the Blind Beggar pub in Whitechapel. Cornell, from the rival South London Richardson Gang, had called Kray a "fat poof." While serving a life sentence for the crime, Kray described the killing in his—and his brother Reg's—book, *Our Story* (1988):

"It was very quiet and gloomy inside the pub. There was an old bloke sitting behind the bar and three people in the saloon bar: two blokes at a table and George Cornell sitting alone at a stool at the far end of the bar. As we walked in the barmaid was putting on a record. It was the Walker Brothers and it was called *The Sun Ain't Gonna Shine Any More*. For George Cornell that was certainly true.

"As we walked towards him he turned around and a sort of sneer came over his face. 'Well, look who's here,' he said.

"I never said anything. I just felt hatred for this sneering man. I took out my gun and held it towards his face. Nothing was said, but his eyes told me he thought the whole thing was a bluff. I shot him in the forehead. He fell forward onto the bar. There was some blood on the counter. That's all that happened . . . It was over very quickly. There was silence. Everyone had disappeared—the barmaid, the old man in the public, and the blokes in the saloon bar. It was like a ghost pub . . .

"I felt f***ing marvellous. I have never felt so good, so bloody alive, before or since. Twenty years on and I can recall every second of the killing of George Cornell. I have replayed it in my mind millions of times."

—————————— HULKS ——————————

BETWEEN 1718 AND 1775, BRITAIN transported 50,000 convicts to her American colonies. The American Revolutionary War ended transportation, and led to a crisis for the British penal system, with prisons rapidly becoming overcrowded. The solution, from 1776, was to use decommissioned warships, called hulks, as floating prisons. Their decks were stripped of masts and rigging, sheds were erected to provide extra accommodation, and the gunports were barred with iron lattices. Hulks were moored off naval bases at Portsmouth, Deptford, and Woolwich. During the day, the men were brought ashore to work in the dockyards. Each convict was fitted with a 14-pound leg iron on his right ankle, to prevent him swimming to freedom.

Hulks were filthy, stinking, wet, overcrowded, and disease-ridden. Although they were only supposed to be a temporary solution to prison overcrowding, they remained in use for 80 years.

ACRONYMS: C

CID: Criminal Investigation Department. British plain clothes detectives branch established in Nottingham in 1854.
CSU: Crime Scene Unit. This is the team that collects the forensics evidence at the scene of a crime.
CSI: Crime Scene Investigator (or investigations).
CPS: The British Crown Prosecution Service is responsible for prosecuting people charged with criminal offences.

THE CON IS ON

THE PERPETRATOR OF A CONFIDENCE trick is often referred to as a confidence (or "con") man, woman, or artist, or a grifter. The first known usage of the phrase "confidence man" was in 1849 by the New York press, during the trial of William Thompson. Thompson chatted with strangers until he asked them if they had the confidence to lend him their watches, which he would promptly walk off with. He was captured when a victim recognized him on the street.

A confidence trick is also known as a con game, a con, a scam, a grift, a hustle, a swindle, a flimflam, or a bamboozle. The intended victims are known as marks or suckers. Con men often rely on the fundamental dishonesty of their victims. The main principle of conning is, "You can't con an honest John," and so they employ the victim's greed to lever success. Confidence tricks also exploit other human frailties, such as vanity, desperation, compassion, credulity, irresponsibility, and naïveté. This means there is no consistent profile of con victims; the common denominator is simply that the victim relies on the good faith of the con artist. In David Mamet's film *House of Games*, the main con artist explains that, in a typical swindle, the con man gives the mark his own confidence, encouraging the mark to in turn trust him. The con artist poses as a trustworthy person looking for another trustworthy person.

The "Golden Age" of the big cons was between 1890–1923 when communications were poorer and documentation was easier to forge, allowing grifters greater credulity, like George Parker, who "sold" the Brooklyn Bridge to unwary tourists twice a week for years. In the most sophisticated cons, the victim never realizes he's been conned. He thinks he was just involved in a failed gamble. More often than not, victims are too embarrassed to report that they've been duped, freeing the con man to repeat the same trick elsewhere.

— CHARLES STARKWEATHER (1938-1959) —

STARKWEATHER DRESSED AND GROOMED HIMSELF to look like
James Dean, with whom he was fixated on. At the age of 18 he meet
13-year-old Caril Ann Fugate and dropped out of high school a year
later. Starkweather killed his first victim, service station attendant
Robert Colvert, on November 30, 1957. Two months later he went on
an indiscriminate killing spree across Nebraska and Wyoming with his
teenage sweetheart. His 11 victims' ages ranged from 2–70. Starkweather
was executed in 1959, and Fugate was paroled in 1976. Many films have
been made based on the exploits of Starkweather and Fugate including
Badlands (1973) and *Natural Born Killers* (1994).

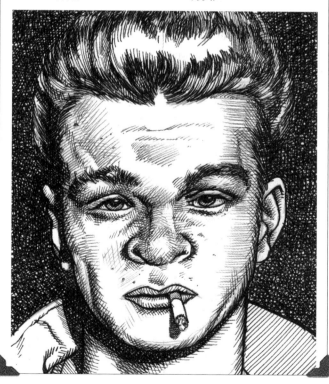

THOMAS JOHN LEY (1880-1947)

SERIAL FRAUDSTER, WARTIME BLACK-MARKETEER and shady businessman, ex-New South Wales' Minister of Justice, Australian Ley moved to the UK with his mistress, Maggie Brook, after a political campaign went disastrously wrong. Ley was linked to two mysterious deaths and a disappearance of a political rival. While in the UK, Ley arranged the death of barman, John McBain Mudie, who Ley wrongly believed was having an affair with Brook. Ley and two of his laborers, including Lawrence John Smith, tortured and killed Mudie. Smith and Ley were sentenced to death in March 1947. Smith's sentence was commuted to life imprisonment, while Ley was declared mad and sent to Broadmoor Asylum for the Criminally Insane, just three days before his scheduled execution. He died in Broadmoor of a meningeal hemorrhage and was said to have been the asylum's wealthiest ever inmate.

EXCELLENT CADAVERS

THE BEST-KNOWN ITALIAN ORGANIZED crime network is the Sicilian Mafia, or Cosa Nostra. Its notoriety stems from its war against the state in the 1980s and 1990s, in which dozens of judges, politicians, prosecutors, policemen, trade union leaders, and journalists were murdered. Public figures who became Mafia victims were called "excellent cadavers."

The assassinations were the work of a ruthless Mafia family from Corleone, led by Salvatore "Totò" Riina. In 1981, Riina began a war against rival Mafia families in Palermo. The Corleonesi wiped out their enemies, and by 1983, Riina had become the supreme Mafia boss.

Riina's last surviving rival was Tomasso Buscetta. After several of his closest relatives, including two sons, had been murdered by Riina, he agreed to become a state witness. Buscetta's testimony led to hundreds of indictments, and the first maxi-trial, in 1986, when 475 Mafiosi appeared in cages in the courtroom in Palermo. The trial, which lasted a year and a half, ended in 344 convictions.

The Mafia response was a wave of assassinations. Among the "excellent cadavers" was Giovanni Falcone, the chief prosecutor, killed by a bomb in 1992, along with his wife and five bodyguards.

In the 1990s, hundreds more Mafia members became *pentiti* (state witnesses). Among them was Salvatore Cancemi, who explained that he had made his decision after hearing Riina say of the *pentiti*, "If it wasn't for them not even the whole world united could touch us. That's why we've got to kill them, and their relatives to the 20th remove, starting with children of six and over."

Riina was eventually betrayed, and arrested on January 15, 1993. Although he had been a fugitive for 23 years, it was revealed that he had been living openly in Palermo, where he had received medical treatment and raised a family.

"The amount of money and of legal energy being given to prosecute hundreds of thousands of Americans who are caught with a few ounces of marijuana in their jeans simply makes no sense—the kindest way to put it. A sterner way to put it is that it is an outrage, an imposition on basic civil liberties and on the reasonable expenditure of social energy."

WILLIAM F. BUCKLEY JR. (1925–2008)
US author, editor, and former CIA employee

> *"To have once been a criminal is no disgrace. To remain a criminal is the disgrace."*
>
> MALCOLM X (1925–1965)
> *US Muslim minister and human rights activist*

THE NECK VERSE

UNTIL THE 19TH CENTURY, convicted felons could escape hanging by pleading "benefit of clergy." This was a legacy of the medieval right of clerics to be tried by ecclesiastical courts, which could not impose the death sentence. The convicted criminal claimed the benefit by reading the first verse of Latin Psalm 51, which begins "Miserere mei Deus: secundum magnam misericordiam tuus" (Have mercy upon me, O God, according to thy loving kindness). This was popularly known as the "Neck Verse."

Benefit of clergy could be claimed only once. To prevent repeated claims, those who received the benefit were branded on the ball of the left thumb. The most famous claimant was Ben Jonson (1572–1637), the English playwright, poet, and actor. In 1598, he killed a fellow actor, Gabriel Spencer, in a duel. Jonson was released, after a short imprisonment, with a branded thumb.

The practice was frequently abused, as illiterate criminals might be taught to memorize the verse, or pay a bystander to prompt them. It was abolished in 1827.

There is an echo of the Neck Verse in modern trials, when a convicted prisoner is asked, "Have you anything to say why the sentence of the court should not be passed upon you?" The historic reason for asking this was to allow the prisoner to claim benefit of clergy. In his 1940 memoirs, the English judge Sir Francis Mackinnon, wrote, "I have heard the modern question many hundred times. The convict, if he answers at all, usually protests that he is really innocent. If any of them ever had the wit to say, 'Yes, I claim my clergy. Give me the book open at the neck verse,' I should have been tempted to knock off a month or two of my intended sentence in recognition of his historical erudition."

MURDEROUS MANNINGS

IN 1849, IN BERMONDSEY, LONDON, Maria Manning, a Swiss French "femme fatale," and her husband, Frederick, murdered her wealthy lover, Patrick O'Connor, in order to rob him. Maria then double-crossed her husband, and fled to Scotland with the loot.

The police discovered O'Connor's naked trussed-up body, buried beneath the Mannings' kitchen floor. Maria was then arrested in Edinburgh, trying to sell a share document stolen from O'Connor. Frederick was caught in Jersey.

Each blamed the other for the murder; both were sentenced to hang. Hearing her sentence, Maria screamed at the jury, "You have treated me like a wild beast of the forest!" Awaiting execution, Frederick confessed, saying that, after his wife shot O'Connor, "He moaned, and I never liked him very well, and I battered in his skull with a ripping chisel."

The double execution of a husband and wife was a rare event, and drew more than 30,000 spectators to the streets outside Horsemonger Lane Prison, where the scaffold was erected. There was a riotous atmosphere, with members of the crowd singing, "Oh! Mrs Manning, don't you cry for me" (to the tune of *Oh! Susanna*). One witness, Charles Dickens, later wrote, "The conduct of the people was so indescribably frightful, that I felt for some time afterwards almost as if I were living in a city of devils."

Among the crowd was another great novelist, Herman Melville, who described the scene in his diary: "Police by hundreds. Men and women fainting. The man and wife were hung side-by-side—still unreconciled to each other. What a change from the time they stood up to be married together! The mob was brutish. All in all, a most wonderful, horrible, and unspeakable scene."

ACRONYMS: D

DWI OR DUI: Driving While Intoxicated or Driving Under the Influence.
DOA: Dead On Arrival.
DA: District Attorney, the elected or appointed official who represents the government in the prosecution of criminal offenses.
DI AND DCI: Detective Inspector and Detective Chief Inspector are ranks in the British police force.
DPP: Director of Public Prosecutions, in charge of the British government's criminal prosecutions via the Crown Prosecution Service.

PRESSED TO DEATH

FROM THE 14TH CENTURY, for a trial to proceed, the accused had to enter a plea of guilty or not guilty. Those who refused to do this were subjected to a form of judicial torture called "peine forte at dure" (hard and forceful punishment). They were pinioned on their backs, with a board resting on their chests, on which stone or iron weights of increasing weight were placed till they agreed to plead or were pressed to death.

Some prisoners, knowing that they faced conviction anyway, chose to die under the weights. This ensured that their families would inherit their property, which would otherwise be forfeited to the Crown. In 1659, Major Strangways, who had murdered his brother-in-law, refused to enter a plea. He invited his friends to attend the pressing in Newgate Prison, and wore mourning clothes. Strangway's friends jumped onto the board to help him die.

During the 1692 witch trials in Salem, Massachusetts, Giles Corey, an 81-year-old farmer, refused to answer the charge of being a warlock. He was pressed to death over two days. Each time Corey was asked to plead, he replied simply, "More weight!" Corey died in possession of his lands, which were inherited by his two sons-in-law.

Pressing was last used in 1741 and abolished in 1777, when refusal to answer a charge was taken as a guilty plea. This was reversed in 1828 and, ever since, refusal to plead has been taken to mean "not guilty."

— HENRI DÉSIRÉ LANDRU (1869-1922) —

BETWEEN 1915 AND 1919 LANDRU preyed on middle-aged women widowed by World War One. He would advertise in lonely heart columns, lure them to his Parisian villa, and seduce them. Once they'd signed over their assets he would stab or strangle them and burn their dismembered bodies in his oven. These 11 murders earned him the moniker of "The French Bluebeard." His final fate was a date with "Madame Guillotine" on February 22, 1922. Landru is listed as one of the waxwork figures in H.P. Lovecraft's short story *The Horror in the Museum*, and his severed head is on display at the Museum of Death in Hollywood, California.

> *"Everyone I know is either dead or in jail. I want to become a boss.
> I want to have supermarkets, stores, factories. I want to have women.
> I want three cars. I want respect when I go into a store. I want to have
> warehouses all over the world. And then I want to die. I want to die
> like a man, someone who truly commands. I want to be killed."*
>
> *Neapolitan juvenile delinquent's letter to a priest,*
> QUOTED BY ROBERTO SAVIANO IN *Gomorrah: Italy's Other Mafia, 2007*

CROSSROADS BURIAL

IN THE PAST, SUICIDES were seen as having committed self-murder, and prevented from receiving a consecrated burial. From the Middle Ages, it was customary to bury people who had killed themselves at the nearest crossroads, with a stake driven though their heart. One theory is that the crossroads location was chosen to confuse the unquiet spirits of the deceased, who would be unable to find the road back to haunt the living. The stake was also used to trap the dead in their grave.

In 1822, the Foreign Secretary, Lord Castlereagh, was given a state funeral in Westminster Abbey, despite having cut his throat with a penknife. There were protests against the funeral, because Castlereagh was a widely hated reactionary. Lord Byron wrote, "Of the manner of his death little need be said, except that if a poor radical had cut his throat, he would have been buried in a crossroad, with the usual appurtenances of the stake and mallet."

It was partly as a result of the controversy surrounding Castlereagh's funeral that the law was changed the following year. The last recorded crossroads burial of a suicide was held near Victoria Station, London, in 1823.

ACRONYMS: E

ECHR: European Convention on Human Rights ensures that basic rights are not infringed by member states and their police forces or individuals. It prohibits the use of torture, and protects the right to privacy and fair trials, among others.

FAREWELL TO TYBURN

IN 1783, THE LONDON AUTHORITIES, worried about the rowdy behavior of the crowds, decided to end the procession to Tyburn and stage hangings outside Newgate Prison. Dr Samuel Johnson did not approve:

> *"The age is running mad after innovation; and all the business of the world is to be done in a new way; men are to be hanged in a new way; Tyburn itself is not safe from the fury of innovation." It having been argued that this was an improvement—"No, Sir, (said he, eagerly,) it is not an improvement; they object, that the old method drew together a number of spectators. Sir, executions are intended to draw spectators. If they do not draw spectators, they don't answer their purpose. The old method was most satisfactory to all parties; the publick was gratified by a procession; the criminal was supported by it. Why is all this to be swept away?"*

(JAMES BOSWELL *The Life of Johnson*, 1787)

ENGIMATIC CRIME

ARGENTINE CON MAN EDUARDO DE VALFIERNO, who claimed to be a Marquis, organized one of the most audacious art heists of all time. In 1911, Valfierno commissioned French art restorer and forger Yves Chaudron to make six copies of the Mona Lisa. The forgeries were then shipped across the world, readying them for the buyers Valfierno had lined up. The Argentine grifter then paid several men to steal the original Mona Lisa from the Louvre. On August 21, museum employee Vincenzo Peruggia hid the painting under his coat and simply walked out the door.

Aware that it would be practically impossible to smuggle the Mona Lisa forgeries out after the theft, Valfierno was one step ahead of customs. After the heist the copies were delivered to their buyers, each believing they had the original, which had been stolen to order for them. Valfierno just wanted to sell the forgeries, and only needed the original Mona Lisa to disappear temporarily. Consequently, he never contacted Peruggia again. Eventually the patsy museum worker, left holding the world's most famous painting, was caught trying to sell it, and Leonardo Da Vinci's masterpiece was eventually returned to the Louvre two years later in 1913.

PEELERS

IN 1829, SIR ROBERT PEEL set up the London Metropolitan Police, the first modern police force. Its members, nicknamed "Bobbies" and "Peelers," wore a uniform of a blue coat with brass buttons, blue trousers, and a black top hat. This was deliberately chosen to resemble the uniform of a Victorian servant rather than a military uniform. The uniform showed that the police were there to serve the public. As a deterrent to crime, the police patrolled the streets at a steady pace, in pairs. Each policeman carried a rattle, to call for help, a wooden truncheon, and a pair of handcuffs.

Although they were popular with the middle and upper classes, Victorian policemen were hated in slum areas, where the locals called them "crushers," "blue locusts," and "blue drones."

By the 1860s, the top hat, which made a perfect target for a thrown brick, had been replaced with a tall helmet, which remains to this day.

LAST WORDS OF DUTCH SCHULTZ

ON OCTOBER 23, 1935, DUTCH SCHULTZ, the New York mobster, was shot by rivals in the Palace Chophouse, Newark, New Jersey. While he lay dying in hospital, his delirious last words were recorded by a police stenographer, "You can play jacks and girls do that with a soft ball and do tricks with it. I take all events into consideration. No. No. And it is no. It is confused and it says no. A boy has never wept nor dashed a thousand kim . . . Police, mamma, Helen, mother, please take me out. I will settle the indictment. Come on, open the soap duckets. The chimney sweeps. Talk to the sword. Shut up, you got a big mouth! Please help me up, Henry. Max, come over here. French-Canadian bean soup. I want to pay. Let them leave me alone."

Schultz's strange last words, resembling stream of consciousness poetry, have inspired several artists and writers, including William Burroughs, who wrote a screenplay, *The Last Words of Dutch Schultz,* in 1970, and the Dutch animator Gerrit van Dijk, who made a film of them in 2003. In the 1975 *Illuminatus Trilogy* of novels by Robert Anton Wilson and Robert Shea, Schultz's words are interpreted as a coded message from a global conspiracy.

LUIGI LUCHENI (1873–1910)

LUCHENI WAS A FRENCH-ITALIAN anarchist who believed in "Propaganda of the Dead," a philosophy advocating violent direct action, and he was determined to go down in history as a martyr of the anarchist movement. Luigi wrote in his journal: "How I would like to kill someone—but it must be someone important so it gets in the papers." He chose Austrian Empress Elisabeth of Bavaria and stabbed her to death in Geneva, Switzerland, with a sharp needle file. He was sentenced to life imprisonment, but hanged himself with his own belt in prison. Parts of his body, including his head, were preserved for scientific purposes.

ANGELO BUONO JNR. (1934-2002)

BUONO, ALONG WITH HIS COUSIN Kenneth Bianchi, started out as pimps before the murder of a prostitute lead to a four-month rape and murder spree between 1977–1978, which claimed a total of 10 lives, in the hills above Los Angeles. In 1979, Bianchi returned to Washington and was subsequently arrested for a double homicide, and in exchange for life imprisonment he gave up his cousin. Buono's trial, which lasted from November 1981 until November 1983 was—at the time—the longest in American legal history. He was eventually convicted of nine counts of first-degree murder and was sentenced to life imprisonment without parole. He died of a heart attack in prison.

MOSTLY ARMLESS

WHEN AN 11-FOOT TIGER shark regurgitated a human arm before a crowd at the Coogee Aquarium Baths, Sydney, Australia, in 1935, it sparked a mystifying case.

The arm had been hacked off with a knife, and its tattoo and fingerprints belonged to small-time criminal James (Jim) Smith—who was last seen telling his wife he was going fishing with Patrick Brady.

Brady and Smith were working a series of insurance scams with local smuggler and fraudster Reginald Holmes. Holmes told police that Brady had turned up at his house with the severed arm demanding £500 and threatening to murder Holmes as well. The wealthy fraudster then threw the arm into the surf.

On the day of Smith's inquest, Holmes was found shot dead in his car, in an apparent suicide—but forensics revealed otherwise. Brady went to trial—but without the rest of Smith's body and the key witness, Holmes, dead—he was found not guilty of murder. Smith's body was never recovered. "The Shark Arm Murders" remain unsolved.

ANIMALS ON TRIAL

IN 1386, AT FALAISE IN FRANCE, a pig was tried and found guilty of murdering a child. The pig, dressed in man's clothes, was hanged in the square by the public executioner.

The case of the pig is one of hundreds collected by the American historian E.P. Evans for his 1906 book, *The Criminal Prosecution and Capital Punishment of Animals: The Lost History of Europe's Animal Trials*. The cases include caterpillars prosecuted for theft, sparrows condemned for chattering in church, and a cock, burned at the stake in Basel in 1474, "For the heinous and unnatural crime of laying an egg."

Evans tells the story of the 16th century French lawyer Bartholomew Chassenée, who made his reputation defending a pack of rats. The rats had been summoned to court, on the charge of destroying the local barley crop. When the rats failed to appear, Chassenée told the court that his clients had been unable to come due to the danger from their mortal enemies, the cats, who lay in wait for them. The case was dropped.

According to the psychologist, Nicholas Humphrey, such court cases were a way of making sense of otherwise meaningless and random acts of destruction, such as the killing of a baby by a pig. In his 1987 introduction to Evans' book, Humphrey writes, "The job of the courts was to domesticate chaos, to impose order on a world of accidents—and specifically to make sense of certain seemingly inexplicable events by redefining them as crimes."

ACRONYMS: F

FBI: Federal Bureau of Investigation. Originally the Bureau Of Investigation in 1901, Director J. Edgar Hoover changed its name in 1935. It has 56 field offices in major cities across the USA.

FST: The acronym for 'field sobriety test' used on suspected drunk drivers. It involves a walking a straight line heel-to-toe or standing on one leg for 30 seconds; and the arresting officer's subjective opinion of impairment.

FTA: An acronym for "failure to appear" to a required court appearance or proceeding.

THE SEPARATE SYSTEM

IN 1829, the US state of Pennsylvania built the Eastern State Penitentiary, which was modeled on a new idea called the "Separate System." To prevent prisoners being a bad influence on each other, they were kept apart in solitary confinement. The design of the prison was later adopted by 300 prisons worldwide, including forty in Britain.

Under the Separate System, the only time prisoners saw each other was in the exercise yard, when they were forced to wear masks to hide their identities. To conceal their identities, they were never addressed by name. Instead, each prisoner wore a badge with a number on it, which they had to answer to as if it was their name.

The convicts' only human contact was with the guards and the prison chaplain, who preached a sermon to them every Sunday. Even in the prison chapel, they were isolated from each other in separate boxes. These prisons were called "penitentiaries" because it was hoped that silent solitary reflection would lead prisoners to penance.

US MAFIA SLANG

BAG MAN: low level Mafia associate sent on errands, such as picking up money

BOOKS: membership rolls of Mafia families

BUTTON: the lowest level member of a Mafia family, also called a "soldier" (as in "foot soldier")

CAPO: a Mafia captain, who heads a small group of soldiers, called a "crew"

CLIP: to kill (also burn, hit, ice, pop, and whack)

COMMISSION: the Mafia leadership, made up of the heads of the most important families

CONSIGLIERE: a trusted Mafia family advisor

CONNECTED: someone who regularly does business with the Mafia, but is not a member of a family

CONTRACT: an order to kill someone

COSA NOSTRA: "our thing," a term for the Mafia, used by members

EARNER: someone who generates income for the Mafia

FAMILY: an organized crime syndicate

FIVE FAMILIES: The five original Mafia families of New York, each named after early bosses: Luchese, Bonanno, Columbo, Gambino, and Genovese

FRIEND OF OURS: shorthand used when introducing one Mafia member to another

FLIP: to become a police informer

MADE: formally inducted into the Mafia through an initiation ceremony. A full Mafia member is a "made guy"

MESSAGE JOB: shooting someone in a particular body part to show others why he was killed, e.g. through the mouth, which indicates that the victim was an informer

OMERTÀ: the Mafia code of silence

RAT: to inform; an informer is also a rat

SKIM: to siphon funds from a legitimate business to the Mafia

SPRING-CLEANING: getting rid of evidence from a crime scene

STAND-UP GUY: a trustworthy man, who will not rat under any circumstances

UNDERBOSS: second-in-command of a Mafia family

WAR: violent conflict between Mafia families

————— 18ᵀᴴ CENTURY CRIMINAL SLANG —————

ADAM-TILER: a lookout

AFFIDAVIT MAN: someone paid to appear in court as a false witness

AUTEM DIVER: a church pickpocket

BUNTER: a prostitute, also called a buttock

BUTTOCK BROKER: a prostitute's madam (bawd or procuress)

BUTTOCK AND FILE: a prostitute who is also a pickpocket

CANTING: slang used by criminals and beggars

CLOAK TWITCHER: a thief who lurks in dark alleys, and steals cloaks from passers-by

CREW: a criminal gang

DARBIES: fetters

FLYING THE BASKET: throwing a boy into the basket of a coach, to toss out the passengers' bags

JACOB: a ladder

HOOK POLE LAY: pulling travelers off horses using long hooked poles

KIMBAW: to beat severely; also to cheat

KING'S HEAD INN: Newgate Prison

LINK BOY: a boy with a lantern paid to light the way down dark streets

MILL: to kill or rob

MILLKEN: a burglar

MOON CURSER: a link boy who robs his customers, or leads them into an ambush

NUBBING: hanging. The neck is called the "nub," the hangman, the "nubbing cove," and the gallows the "nubbing cheat"

NUT CRACKERS: the pillory

PEACH: to betray to the authorities (short for impeach)

RATTLING LAY: to steal from coaches

RIPPING COVE: a burglar who breaks into a house by ripping the tiles from the roof

SCRAGGED: hanged

YELLOW BOY: a guinea (a gold coin)

ROBERT BLACK (1947-)

SCOTTISH BLACK WAS ARRESTED IN 1990 and convicted of the kidnapping, sexual assault, and murder of four girls. The psychopathic Black is also suspected of a number of unsolved child murders dating back to 1969 throughout the UK and Europe. Currently serving 11 life sentences, Black was told he would be at least 89 years old before he would be considered for parole.

DNA PROFILING

D NA IS THE UNIQUE GENETIC code possessed by every individual, apart from identical twins. In 1984-5, a British scientist, Sir Alec Jeffreys, developed DNA profiling, a way to extract the code from human cells left at a crime scene. DNA can be obtained from blood, semen, hair, saliva, mucus, perspiration, and even old stains.

In 1983 and 1986, two 15-year-old schoolgirls were raped and murdered in Leicestershire. Richard Buckland, a 17-year-old with a learning disability, confessed to the second murder. By comparing Buckland's DNA, taken from a blood sample, with DNA from the killer's semen, Jeffreys proved that Buckland was innocent.

In 1987, the police investigating the murders carried out the first mass DNA screening, taking blood and saliva samples from 5,000 local men. The process took six months, but the killer was not found.

Soon after, a man called Ian Kelly was overheard boasting in a pub that he had impersonated a workmate, Colin Pitchfork, during the mass screening. Pitchfork was arrested, and it was discovered from his DNA that he was guilty of the murders. He was sentenced to life imprisonment.

Since 1989, hundreds of criminals have been convicted, and hundreds of convicted criminals exonerated, thanks to DNA profiling. DNA has also been used to solve cold cases.

One of the last men to be hanged in Britain was James Hanratty, convicted in 1962 for the murder of Michael Gregston and the rape and attempted murder of his mistress, Valerie Storey. The evidence against Hanratty was weak, and his family campaigned for years to have his conviction overturned. In 2002, his body was exhumed, and his DNA was compared with a sample of 40-year-old mucus from a handkerchief in which the murder weapon had been wrapped. It was Hanratty's DNA on the handkerchief. Lord Woolf, the Lord Chief Justice, announced that this was "overwhelming proof of the safety of the conviction."

ACRONYMS: G

GBH: Grievous Bodily Harm. UK legal term for "wounding with intent" or "malicious wounding."
GTA: Grand Theft Auto. US legal term for stealing a car. Brought to popularity by the series of computer games of the same name.

> *"There are crimes of passion and crimes of logic.*
> *The boundary between them is not clearly defined."*
> ALBERT CAMUS (1913–1960)
> *French Pied-Noir author, journalist, and philosopher*

TYBURN TREE

FROM 1196 UNTIL 1783, London's main execution site was Tyburn, to the west of the city. Executions took place eight to ten times a year on special "Hanging Mondays," which were public holidays. From 1571, there was a permanent triangular gallows, with three cross beams, nicknamed the "Tyburn Tree." It was 18 feet high, and big enough to hang 24 people, with eight on each beam.

On Hanging Mondays the condemned were taken by carts on a three-mile journey from Newgate Prison to Tyburn. They were guarded by some 200 mounted marshalmen, armed with pikes. The procession stopped at taverns along the route where the prisoners drank and greeted their friends. The whole route was packed with onlookers, including women throwing bunches of flowers to the most celebrated criminals. Unpopular prisoners were insulted and pelted with rubbish.

The biggest crowds gathered at Tyburn itself, where stands were erected above the gallows to give the public a much better view. Here, the prisoner was placed on another carriage and driven beneath the gallows. They might make a final speech, before the noose was placed around their neck, and the horses jerked forward.

With a short rope and no drop, death followed by slow strangulation. Friends often stood beneath the gallows, where they would pull on the condemned's legs to shorten their suffering.

People often rushed forward to touch the corpse's hand. It was popularly believed that contact with a hanged corpse could cure skin diseases and other ailments.

London's surgeons had the right to 10 executed corpses a year, for public dissection. When the surgeons' agents arrived to claim their corpse, they of had to fight for it with the fami friends of the deceased. C feared the prospect of be more than the gallows

PETER MANUEL (1927-1958)

"THE BEAST OF BIRKENSHAW" was born in New York City, but immigrated to the UK in 1932. He is known to have shot seven victims, bludgeoned one with an iron bar, and strangled a ninth, but confessed to 18 murders in total between 1956–1958. After killing his last three victims, Peter, Doris, and Michael Smart, Manuel lived in their house for nearly a week eating leftovers and even looking after their cat. He stole their car and picked up a policeman whom he told was looking in the wrong place for the killer of his previous victim, 17-year-old Isabelle Cooke. His spree across Lanarkshire and Southern Scotland was finally stopped when he was found in possession of money that he'd stolen from the Smarts. He was hanged on July 11, 1958.

THE HUMAN FLY AND THE CAT

PETER SCOTT, nicknamed "the human fly," was a profesional cat burglar, who specialized in robbing rich houses in Mayfair, London, and on the French Riviera. In his 1995 autobiography, *Gentleman Thief: The Recollections of a Cat Burglar*, he boasted that, over a 35-year career, he had stolen £30 million in jewelry. His victims included the actress Sophia Loren, whose jewels he stole when she was filming *The Millionairess* at Elstree in 1960.

In 1998, the 67-year-old Scott, who claimed he had retired from crime, was sentenced to three and a half years for taking part in the theft of a Picasso painting. As the sentence was handed down, an 81-year-old man, who introduced himself to the court as "Ray the Cat," denounced Scott as a liar for claiming sole credit for the Sophia Loren robbery. Ray "the Cat" Jones, a fellow cat burglar, had been outraged by Scott's book. He claimed it was he who broke into Loren's room to steal her jewelry, while the Human Fly merely acted as look-out.

In 1997, the Cat sold his own story to the Irish *Sunday World*, in which

he boasted of also robbing Elizabeth Taylor. He said he had turned to burglary after being imprisoned on a false charge, "I got on my knees in my prison cell. I vowed I would hit back at society and the judiciary for taking the things I cared most about in life away from me. When I got out, I said to myself, I would become the greatest cat burglar in the world. That was my mission in life . . . I would only hit rich people. They were the cream of the crop and had every-thing they wanted. I had been robbed of my life. I had to hit back."

"I'm tired of gang wars and gang shootings . . . You fear death and worse than death . . . Three of my friends were killed in Chicago last week. That certainly doesn't give you peace of mind. I haven't had peace of mind in years. Even on a peace errand you're taking a chance on the light suddenly going out."

AL CAPONE (1899–1947) US gangster

ACRONYMS: H

HMP: Her Majesty's Prison. Every British jail has this prefix before its name. Criminals are said to be incarcerated "at her Majesty's pleasure."
HP: Highway Patrol. This suffix is used after most States' traffic police department, e.g. The California Highway Patrol is CHP.

THE MAN WITH 1,000 FACES

JACQUES MESRINE (1936–1979) WAS A notorious French criminal whose 25-year career included numerous robberies, murders, and prison escapes. His love of disguise earned him the nickname "The man with 1,000 faces."

Mesrine came to the media's attention in Canada, in 1969, when he was sentenced to 10 years in prison, following a bungled kidnapping. In August 1972, he escaped from the high security prison with a fellow convict. The pair then robbed a series of Montreal banks, sometimes two on the same day. In September, they returned to the prison, making an unsuccessful attempt to stage a mass breakout. In the shoot-out, two guards were seriously wounded.

Mesrine returned to France, where he became a national celebrity following a series of bank robberies, kidnappings, and escapes. In September 1973, he was caught and sentenced to 20 years in the Santé prison in Paris. While in prison, Mesrine wrote his autobiography, in which he said, "Some people like golf or skiing. My relaxation is armed robbery." He also blamed his crimes on the French state: "If I have rubbed the word pity from my vocabulary, it is because I have seen so many injustices."

In 1978, Mesrine escaped from the Santé prison. While on the run he gave a series of interviews, telling *Paris Match*, "I will never surrender. Now it is war."

Mesrine was finally killed in a police ambush in Paris, on November 2, 1979, when he was shot 16 times at close range. In a taped last testament, left for his mistress, he said, "What is terrible is that some people will try to make me into a hero and there are no heroes in crime. There are just men out on the edge who do not respect the law."

> *"Crime is naught but misdirected energy."*
> EMMA GOLDMAN (1869–1940) *Russian anarchist and writer*

FRANZ MULLER (1840-1864)

ON JULY 9, 1864, MULLER, a German tailor, beat City banker Thomas Briggs onboard a moving train and threw him off. Briggs died of his brutal injuries shortly after being discovered by another train driver. It was the first murder committed on a British train, and would see the introduction of the now-ubiquitous communication cord. After the crime, Muller fled to the United States, but was arrested by Scotland Yard on his arrival in New York and extradited back to Britain. He received a death sentence by public hanging outside Newgate Prison, pulling in 50,000 spectators. A good crowd for one of the UK's last public hangings.

RATCLIFF HIGHWAY MURDERS

A ROUND MIDNIGHT ON DECEMBER 7, 1811, Timothy Marr, a linen draper, with his wife, apprentice, and baby son, were all brutally murdered in their home on the Ratcliff Highway in East London. The victims had their heads smashed, and the baby's throat was also cut. The killer, or killers, left behind a shipwright's maul, or hammer, caked with blood and hair.

Twelve nights later, there was a second attack, at the nearby King's Arms Tavern. A lodger, John Turner, escaped from the upper floor shouting, "Murder! Murder!" The victims were John Williamson, the publican, his wife, and their servant, who had their heads crushed with an iron crowbar and their throats cut.

The murders created the first national crime panic. Across England, people felt they were not safe in their own homes.

Suspicion fell on John Williams, a sailor who had been drinking in the King's Arms on the night of the second set of murders. The maul was identified as having come from Williams' lodgings. Williams was arrested but, before he could be tried, he hanged himself in his cell. Though there was no hard evidence against him, his suicide was taken as a confession.

Williams' corpse was placed on a tilted board on a cart, with his right leg manacled, and the maul and crowbar placed beside his head. The cart was taken in procession to the two murder sites, and then to the nearest cross-roads, where Williams was thrown into a shallow grave. Using the maul, a stake was hammered through his heart—which was then the way of burying suicides.

In 1886, workmen laying a gas pipe dug up Williams' skeleton. The bones were shared out as souvenirs, and the skull ended up on display behind the bar of the Crown and Dolphin pub.

"[Infrequent or casual drug users] ought to be taken out and shot."
DARYL GATES (1926–2010)
Chief of the Los Angeles Police Department, 1978–1992

JOINING COSA NOSTRA

JOE VALACHI WAS THE FIRST Mafia member to break the code of silence, testifying before a televised Senate subcommittee. *The New York Times,* reported the event on October 2, 1963:

Valachi said he had been taken into a large room where 30 or 35 men were sitting at a long table. "There was a gun and a knife on the table," Valachi testified, "I sat at the edge. They sat me next to Maranzano. I repeated some words in Sicilian after him, 'You live by the gun and knife and die by the gun and knife.'" The witness said Maranzano had then given him a piece of paper that was set alight in his hand. "I repeated in Sicilian, 'This is the way I burn if I betray the organization.'" The witness then said the men around the table each "threw out a number," with each man holding up any number of fingers from one to five. The total was taken. Starting with Maranzano, the sum was then counted off around the table. The man on whom the final number fell was designated as Valachi's godfather. Valachi said the lot had fallen to Bonnano. The witness said that he then had his finger pricked by a needle held by Bonnano to show that he was united to Bonnano by blood. Valachi said he was given two rules in Cosa Nostra that night—one concerning allegiance to it, and another a promise not to possess another member's wife, sister, or daughter. For the first time, the witness grew grim. "This is the worst thing I can do, to tell about the ceremony," he said. "This is my doom, telling it to you and press."

ACRONYMS: I

IA: Internal Affairs. The US police department that investigates police corruption or professional misconduct.
ICPO: International Criminal Police Organization (AKA Interpol).
IPCC: Independent Police Complaints Commission. This body investigates any improprieties within the British police force.

FEELING CRANKY

"TURNING THE CRANK" was a form of hard labor, used in Victorian prisons. The crank was a machine with a handle, which turned paddles in a metal drum holding sand. The prisoner was expected to turn the handle 10,000 or more times a day, and every turn was recorded on a dial. Failure to complete the task resulted in punishments, such as being put on a diet of bread and water. The warder could make the task more difficult by tightening a screw. This is thought to be the origin of the nickname "screw" for a prison officer.

Turning the crank was a deliberately pointless activity, designed to make the punishment even harder to bear. Convicts could not even comfort themselves with the idea that their work was useful.

THE GREAT ESCAPER

THE MOST FAMOUS CRIMINAL of the 18th century was Jack Sheppard (1702–1724). He was celebrated not for his crimes but for the four daring escapes he made from London prisons. Sheppard was the first working-class hero.

Between February and August 1723, Sheppard was arrested three times for theft, each time escaping from captivity. On September 9, he was caught again and locked in the strongest room in Newgate Prison, handcuffed and fitted with leg irons chained to the floor. On the night of October 14, he made his final, and most famous, escape. Using a nail, he picked the locks on his handcuffs and the padlock fastening his leg irons to the floor. After breaking into the chimney, he climbed to a disused room above. Still wearing his leg irons, in pitch darkness, Sheppard broke through six iron doors to reach the prison roof. He then returned all the way to his cell to fetch his blanket, which he used to lower himself to freedom.

Sheppard loved his fame and could not resist returning to the city taverns. On October 31, he was arrested in a gin shop, while dead drunk. The jailors loaded him with 300 lbs of irons, and kept him under constant watch. A huge celebrity, Sheppard received hundreds of visitors, who paid an entrance fee to see him. He boasted, "I am the Sheppard and all the jailors in the town are my flock, and I cannot stir into the country but they are all at my heels."

On November 16, 1724, 200,000 Londoners turned out to see Sheppard hanged at Tyburn. His small frame, which had helped him in his escapes, meant that his execution was a lingering one. *The Newgate Calendar* grimly recorded, "He died with difficulty, and was much pitied by the surrounding multitude."

EUGÈNE DIEUDONNÉ (1884-1944)

EUGÈNE DIEUDONNÉ WAS A PRINCIPLE member of the French Bonnot Gang of anarchist robbers who pioneered the use of cars as getaway vehicles. All members of the gang were vegetarians who only drank water, and their reign of terror lasted from 1911 until their final bloody gun battle with 300 police officers and 800 soldiers in May 1912. Despite claiming only to have been a driver and not one of the robbers, Eugene was convicted of armed robbery and murder, and sentenced to death. However, this was commuted to life imprisonment. He was sent to the French penal colony at Cayenne in Guyana. He escaped on December 6, 1926, was recaptured, and was finally pardoned and returned to France as a cabinet-maker.

—— CORAL EUGENE WATTS (1953-2007) ——

"THE SUNDAY MORNING SLASHER" was first arrested in 1969 for sexual assault. Watts began killing in 1974 and by 1982 had murdered over a dozen women—strangling, stabbing, bludgeoning, and drowning them in Michigan, Texas, and Canada. Following his arrest, Texas authorities offered Watts a plea bargain, giving him immunity from the murder charges, if he confessed. He took the deal and confessed to 12 murders in Texas and was charged with "burglary with intent to murder." Watts claimed to have killed 40 women and implied that there were more than 80 in total. The authorities considered Watts a suspect in at least 90 unsolved murders. However the Michigan authorities wouldn't agree to the plea bargain. Convicted and sentenced to 60 years in prison, commuted to life imprisonment without parole in Texas and two life sentences in Michigan, he eventually died of prostate cancer in a Jackson, MI hospital. He had a reported I.Q. of 75.

ACRONYMS: J

JD: Juvenile Delinquent. Description of any criminal under legal adult age (18 in most countries).

CUTPURSE SCHOOL

IN 1585, THERE WAS A school for young cutpurses in an alehouse in Billingsgate, London. It was run by an ex-merchant called Wotton, who had decorated the walls with mottos, such as, "Lift, Shave, and Spare Not." According to a letter written by William Fleetwood, the senior London judge, Wotton trained his pupils using a pocket and a purse:

"The pocket had in it certain counters, and was hung about with hawk's bells, and over the top did hang a little sacring bell; and he that could take out a counter without any noise was allowed to be a Public Foister; and he that could take a piece of silver off the purse without the noise of any of the bells, he was adjudged a Judicial Nipper."

TONG WARS

IN THE 19TH CENTURY, Chinese immigrants in America formed mutual support organizations, called Tongs, from a word meaning "hall" or "gathering place." Many tongs raised money through gambling and opium, activities that were tolerated in China but illegal in the US. Some also organized prostitution and collected protection money from members of the Chinese community.

As the tongs grew more powerful, violent conflicts broke over territory in larger cities such as New York and San Francisco. In the early 1900s, there were a series of tong wars in New York's Chinatown, when the dominant On Leong tong, led by Tom Lee, was challenged by the Hip Sings, led by Sai Wing Mock, known as "Mock Duck." The crime journalist Herbert Asbury described Mock Duck in *The Gangs of New York* (1928):

"He wore a suit of chain mail with which all of the tong killers of the period protected their precious bodies, he carried two guns and a hatchet, and at times he would fight bravely, squatting on his haunches in the street with both eyes shut, and blazing away at the surrounding circle of On Leongs with an utter disregard of his own safety. At other times Mock Duck got the wind up, and fled pell mell to San Francisco or Chicago—but he always came back, filled with new schemes for the discomfiture of the On Leongs."

The Tong Wars inspired a 1932 Hollywood film called *The Hatchet Man,* the name given to the hired assasins that the tongs would employ, also known as "boo how doy." It is believed they favored hatchets for weapons. Directed by William A. Wellman, all the main roles were controversially played by white Americans. The film starred Edward G. Robinson as Wong Low Get, a leading tong killer, Loretta Young as the beautiful heroine, Sun Toya San, and Leslie Fenton as Harry En Hai, the love rival.

PIERRE CHANAL (1946-2003)

COMMITTING SUICIDE DURING HIS TRIAL in 2003 meant that Chanal was never convicted of his crimes for which he was charged. Chanal was a French commando-trained army vet who rose to the rank of Sergeant Major in the 4th Dragoons Regiment. Chanal had been convicted of an early crime of kidnapping and raping a young Hungarian male hitchhiker in 1988 and was released on probation in 1995. Investigators believed he might have murdered an additional eight young men in the 1980s, who all disappeared in the north-east region of Marne, France—seven of the bodies have never been found. Most of the missing men were army conscripts stationed at Mourmelon, the same camp as Chanal.

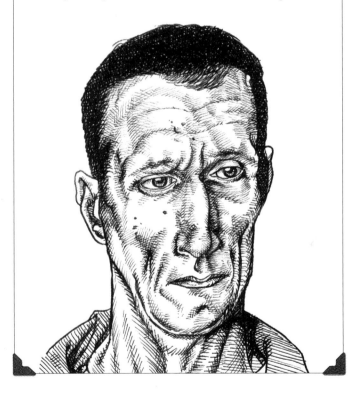

———— VICTORIAN CRIMINAL SLANG ————

AREA DIVING: sneaking into the lower ground floor servants' entrance to a house (the area), and stealing from the kitchen

BARKER: a pistol

BILLY: a handkerchief (usually a silk one, valued by pickpockets)

BOAT, GET THE: to be sentenced to transportation to Australia

CHIV, OR SHIV: a knife

CRACKSMAN: a burglar or safe-cracker

CROAK: to die

DEAD LURK, A: breaking into a house while the family have gone to church

DRAGSMAN: thief who climbs on top of carriages, and cuts the straps that secure the luggage

FAMILY PEOPLE: term used by thieves to refer to themselves

FILCH: to steal

FLASH HOUSE: a pub used by criminals to plan jobs or arrange the sale of stolen goods

FLOATING ACADEMY: hulk (disused warship used as a prison)

FLYING THE BLUE PIGEON: stealing lead from roofs

GILT: money

GONOPH: a thief or pickpocket (originally a Yiddish word)

KIDSMAN: organizer of a gang of child thieves

LAGGED: to be sentenced to penal servitude

MAGSMAN: a low level cheat. A "mag" is a halfpence

MALTOOLER: a pickpocket who steals from other passengers while riding on a horse drawn bus

MOBSMAN: a well-dressed pickpocket or swindler

MUTCHER: a thief who steals from drunks

NIBBED: arrested

NOMMUS!: get away quick!

PALMER: a shoplifter

PETER: a box, trunk, or safe

PUSH: money

SCALDRUM DODGE: begging with the help of self-inflicted, or feigned, wounds

SCREW: to break into

SCROBY: a prison flogging, also called "claws for breakfast"

SHIN SCRAPER: a prison treadmill

SMASHING QUEER SCREENS: passing forged banknotes

SNIDE: counterfeit (money or jewelry)

SNOOZER: a thief who booked into a hotel and then robbed the other rooms while the guests were sleeping

SNOWING: stealing laundry left out to dry

STALL: a thief's accomplice who gets in the way of pursuers

STICKMAN: a pickpocket's accomplice, who receives the stolen goods

SWAG: booty from a robbery

TOOLER: a pickpocket

TOPPED: hanged (also stretched)

──── DAVID BERKOWITZ (1953-) ────

BERKOWITZ'S NEW YORK KILLING SPREE began in the summer of 1976 and lasted for just over a year. Shooting his 15 victims with a .44 Bulldog revolver, and killing six of them, Berkowitz taunted the authorities with letters promising further murders, calling himself "Son of Sam." So intense was the search for him that even the Mafia put its "soldiers" onto the streets looking for him. He was eventually caught on August 10, 1977 stating, "Well, you got me. How come it took you such a long time?" After his arrest, Berkowitz confessed to all the crimes and claimed that he had been commanded to kill by his neighbor's dog, Harvey, who was possessed by a demon—he later retracted this as a hoax. He was convicted of murder in the second degree and attempted murder in the second degree and is currently serving six consecutive life sentences. After concerns that Berkowitz might profit from book deals, the "Son of Sam laws" were passed to prevent criminals from gaining financially from their crimes.

THIEF-TAKERS

IN 1693, THE BRITISH government offered a reward of £40 for anybody who captured a thief and secured his or her conviction. At the same time, the growth of newspapers allowed victims of crime to advertise rewards for the return of stolen property. Both rewards led to the appearance of the first private "thief-takers," who resembled modern US bounty hunters.

Thief-taking offered ample opportunities to the unscrupulous. Thief-takers often worked hand-in-hand with thieves, acting as fences and brokers for the return of stolen goods. The most notorious was Jonathan Wild (1683–1725) who styled himself "Thief-Taker General of Great Britain and Ireland." In fact, Wild was a criminal mastermind who controlled the London underworld from his headquarters opposite Newgate Prison.

Wild cultivated the public image of a brave and resourceful thief-taker, boasting that he had sent more than 60 criminals to the gallows. Between 1721 and 1723, Wild broke up the three largest criminal gangs in London. In a series of violent gang wars, he was wounded 19 times, and his fractured skull was held together with silver plates.

While posing as a policeman, Wild was in fact organizing robberies through his own criminal gangs, often taking part in the thefts in person. The thieves he prosecuted were those who refused to work for him, or who had outlived their usefulness.

Wild made many powerful enemies, who quickly turned on him after he was arrested in 1725 for receiving stolen goods.

Sentenced to hang, and suffering from gout and insanity, he attempted suicide by drinking laudanum on the day of his execution, but vomitted it back up. He was pelted with rubbish during his procession to Newgate. After his hanging at the gallows in Tyburn, his body was dissected and Wild's skeleton can still be seen on display at the Hunterian Museum in the Royal College of Surgeons in London.

ACRONYMS: K

KGB: Komitet Gosudarstvennoy Bezopasnosti. The Russian state security agency that replaced the NKVD and operated between 1954–1991.
K&A: Knock and Announce. This is the required communication that all US police officers must supply when serving a search warrant.

—————— MARY ANN COTTON ——————

THE MOST PROLIFIC VICTORIAN POISONER was a poor Durham woman called Mary Ann Cotton (1832–73), who was hanged for using arsenic to murder her stepson. It is thought that she also killed between 14 and 20 other people, including three husbands, a lover, a friend, and several children. Her motive was to collect insurance money.

After her execution, Mary Ann lived on in a children's skipping song, which is still sung in North East England:

Mary Ann Cotton,
Dead and forgotten
She lies in her bed,
With her eyes wide open
Sing, sing, oh, what can I sing,
Mary Ann Cotton is tied up with string
Where, where? Up in the air
Sellin' black puddens a penny a pair.
Mary Ann Cotton
She's dead and forgotten,
She lies in a grave with her bones all-rotten

—————— THE ICEMAN CONFESSES ——————

RICHARD "THE ICEMAN" Kuklinski (1935–2006) was a cold-blooded contract killer for the US Mafia, who admitted to murdering more than 100 people between 1948–86. In prison, in 1991, he was interviewed by HBO: "There was a man who was begging, and pleading, and praying, I guess. He was 'Please God-ing' all over the place. So I told him he could have a half hour to pray to God, and if God could come down and change the circumstances, he'd have that time.

"But God never showed up and he never changed the circumstances, and that was that. It wasn't too nice."

—————— ACRONYMS: L ——————

LPR: License Plate Recognition. Mass surveillance system that uses optical character recognition.

THOMAS QUICK (1950-)

SWEDISH QUICK, A COMPULSIVE LIAR, was originally convicted of armed robbery. While incarcerated, Quick—real name, Sture Bergwall—began confessing to dozens of unsolved murders across Scandinavia, some going back to 1964 when Quick was only 14. He ultimately confessed to the murder of over 30 people and he was subsequently convicted of eight, despite the lack of any physical evidence. In 2008, Quick, now using his real name once again, withdrew all of his confessions, and in 2010 he was finally acquitted on all counts of murder. This is one of the most controversial cases in Swedish law where a compulsive liar has remained incarcerated in a psychiatric hospital for the criminally insane for over 20 years for crimes he may or may not have committed.

——————————— JOE BANANAS ———————————

FOR 30 YEARS, JOSEPH BONANNO (1905–2002), nicknamed "Joe Bananas," was the godfather of a Brooklyn crime family. In his revelatory 1983 book, *A Man of Honour: The Autobiography of a Godfather*, he explained the meaning of *Omertà*:

"*Omertà* comes from the word 'omu' or 'omo'—which means, 'man.' In my Tradition, omertà has come to describe the manly behavior of someone who refuses to get his friends in trouble.

"In the hands of the police, a captive from our Tradition ideally should remain silent. He should not cooperate. Such a man is willing to face even death, rather than betray his friends to the authorities, or to his rivals. Omertà in my Tradition is a noble principle. It praises silence and scorns the informer.

"Try as you might, there's no complimentary way of describing an informer. All the terms are pejorative: stool pigeon, spy, rat, tattler, quisling, fifth-columnist, betrayer."

——————————— TAXI WARS ———————————

SINCE THE LATE 1980S, there has been a series of "taxi wars" in South Africa. Around 60 percent of South African commuters travel to work in taxis, mostly in 16-seater minibuses. There are big profits to be made by transporting them, and there is fierce competition over routes.

Until 1987—when the industry was deregulated—taxis were a government monopoly. As a result of deregulation, rival taxi cartels appeared, which employed hundreds of poor blacks to drive their minibuses. As the competition over routes intensified, the cartels hired gunmen to shoot rival drivers. Between 1991 and 1999, more than 2,000 South Africans were killed in the taxi wars.

In 2006, the *New York Times* reported on a typical war, fought between the Congress for Democratic Taxi Associations (Codeta) and the Cape Amalgamated Taxi Association (Cata): "The latest surge in Cape Peninsula killings . . . can be traced to the opening of a shopping mall near Kraaifontein, a Cape Town suburb, which employs many workers from Khayelitsha, in the south. Codeta taxis want to take the workers directly to the mall. Cata officials insist that the approved route runs through a taxi stand at Bellville which they dominate, and that the passengers must transfer to their taxis there.

"'If you try to operate from Bellville to Kraaifontein, then your vehicle is shot at and your passengers are intimidated,' said Mangalisa Nakani, the secretary of Codeta."

ACRONYMS: M

MP: Military Police are responsible for policing within armies.
MTU: Mobile Tactical Unit
MI5: Stands for Military Intelligence, Section 5, the department of the British Intelligence Service that provides internal security and handles counter-intelligence.

HIGHWAYMEN

18TH CENTURY CRIMINALS SAW themselves as belonging to a professional hierarchy, with highwaymen at the top. Highwaymen, who robbed coaches on horseback, were proud to be nicknamed "Gentlemen of the road."

James O'Brien, a 20-year-old highwayman hanged in 1730, said that he "Thought it below him to commit petty thefts, such as pick-pocketing, but thought it more becoming a manly spirit to attack coaches, and such people as he met upon the highway."

Highwaymen often dressed as dandies. The most flamboyant was John Rann (1750–1774), nicknamed "Sixteen String Jack" from the multicolored silk ribbons that he wore on the knees of his breeches. Rann was arrested and tried seven times, and acquitted six times for lack of evidence.

Rann's biography, written by the Newgate Ordinary (chaplain), is like an article on Georgian fashion. In 1774, he appeared at the Barnet horse races dressed "Like a sporting peer of the first rank . . . in a blue satin waistcoat laced with silver, and was followed by hundreds from one side of the course to the other, whose curiosity was excited to behold a genius, whose exploits were so notorious to the world."

On the night before his execution, the Ordinary recorded that "Not less than seven girls dined with him; the company was very cheerful, and the wicked culprit appeared quite insensible to the dreadful situation his crimes have brought him."

James Boswell was one of the thousands of members of the public who went to Tyburn to see Sixteen String Jack hanged to death. Boswell recorded that the fashionable highwayman "Was cheered by the whole vagabond population of London."

OLD BILL

OFTEN REFERRED TO AS THE "Old Bill," London's Metropolitan Police themselves seem unable to pinpoint the origins of this nickname. There are at least 13 different theories, including: named after the music hall song, *Won't You Come Home, Bill Bailey*; after the bills, or billhooks, officers carried as weapons; or after the popular Sergeant Bill Smith, based in Limehouse in the 1860s. However, the most likely is that after World War One many police officers sported large moustaches, similar to the one popularized by Bruce Bairnsfather's cartoon trench solider, "Old Bill." In 1917 the British government used Bairnsfather's character in propaganda campaign, under the heading "Old Bill says . . . " with the character dressed in a special constable's uniform. The name stuck and is still used colloquially to this day.

THE PERFECT MURDER

IN HIS ESSAY *The Decline of the English Murder*, George Orwell wrote of the British Sunday ritual of reading about murders in the paper and described the ideal story: "The murderer should be a little man of the professional class—a dentist or a solicitor, say—living an intensely respectable life somewhere in the suburbs, and preferably in a semi-detached house, which will allow the neighbors to hear suspicious sounds through the wall. He should be either chairman of the local Conservative Party branch, or a leading Nonconformist and strong Temperance advocate. He should go astray through cherishing a guilty passion for his secretary or the wife of a rival professional man, and should only bring himself to the point of murder after long and terrible wrestles with his conscience. Having decided on murder, he should plan it all with the utmost cunning, and only slip up over some tiny unforeseeable detail. The means chosen should, of course, be poison. In the last analysis he should commit murder because this seems to him less disgraceful, and less damaging to his career, than being detected in adultery."

> *"A successful lawsuit is the one worn by a policeman."*
> ROBERT FROST (1874–1963) *American poet*

STACKOLEE SHOT BILLY

ON CHRISTMAS NIGHT, 1895, a quarrel broke out between a black pimp called "Stack" Lee Shelton and his friend William Lyons in a saloon in St Louis. The *St Louis Globe Democrat* reported (misspelling Shelton's name), "The discussion drifted to politics, and an argument was started, the conclusion of which was that Lyons snatched Sheldon's hat from his head. The latter indignantly demanded its return. Lyons refused, and Sheldon withdrew his revolver and shot Lyons in the abdomen. When his victim fell to the floor Sheldon took his hat from the hand of the wounded man and coolly walked away."

"Stack" Lee later died in prison of tuberculosis. But his name lived on in a song. These are the lyrics recorded by Mississippi John Hurt in 1928:

> *Police officer, how can it be?*
> *You can arrest everybody but cruel Stackolee*
> *That bad man, old, cruel Stackolee.*
> *Billy Lyon told Stackolee, "Please don't take my life, I got two little babies,*
> *and a darling loving wife."*
> *He's a bad man, old, cruel Stackolee.*
> *"What I care about your two little babies, your darling lovin' wife?*
> *Ya done stole my Stetson hat, I'm bound to take your life."*
> *That bad man, old cruel Stack O' Lee.*

Shelton, renamed "Stagolee" or "Stackolee," evolved into a black folk hero and symbol of rebellion against white supremacy. In later versions of the story, Stackolee caused the San Francisco earthquake, and won a duel with the devil.

"The Newgate Calendar, *or* Malefactors' Bloody Register, *containing: Genuine and Circumstantial Narrative of the lives and transactions, various exploits, and Dying Speeches of the Most Notorious Criminals of both sexes who suffered Death Punishment in Gt. Britain and Ireland for High Treason, Petty Treason, Murder, Piracy, Felony, Thieving, Highway Robberies, Forgery, Rapes, Bigamy, Burglaries, Riots, and various other horrid crimes and misdemeanors on a plan entirely new, wherein will be fully displayed the regular progress from virtue to vice, interspersed with striking reflections on the conduct of those unhappy wretches who have fallen a sacrifice to the laws of their country."*

—TITLE PAGE OF THE FIRST NEWGATE CALENDAR, *published in 1773*

—HAMILTON HOWARD "ALBERT" FISH—
(1870-1936)

THE TERRIFYING "ALBERT" FISH (AKA The Gray Man, the Werewolf of Wysteria, and the Brooklyn Vampire) boasted he'd molested and tortured over 100 children, confessed to three murders that police were able to trace, and was the suspect in at least five other killings. He also confessed to stabbing at least two other people. He suffered from mental illness, sadomasochistic tendencies, and indulged in cannibalism. Fish was finally caught in 1934 and convicted of grand larceny, theft, and the murder of 10-year-old Grace Budd. Executed by electric chair, his last words were reported as, "I don't even know why I'm here."

CRIPS AND BLOODS

IN 1971, TWO BLACK TEENAGERS, Raymond Washington and Stanley Tookey Williams, formed a gang in South Central Los Angeles. Their aim was to protect their neighborhood from larger gangs and from police brutality. Due to their youthfulness, they called themselves the Avenue Cribs. This later changed into "Crips," short for "cripples," after members began carrying canes. The Crips also adopted the color blue, in tribute to a murdered member, Curtis Buddha Morrow, who always wore a blue bandana in the back left pocket of his jeans.

Williams and Washington recruited other gangs, by challenging their leaders to fist fights, which they usually won. As the Crips grew more powerful, a rival Los Angeles gang emerged, who called themselves the Bloods. In opposition to the Crips, they adopted the color red. Each gang used hand signs to identify members. Crips formed a letter "C" using the forefinger and thumb. The Bloods identified themselves with signs spelling "Blood" or "CK," standing for "Crip Killer."

The rivalry between the Crips and the Bloods became increasingly violent. Washington, who hated firearms, lost control of the Crips and, in 1979, he was killed in a drive-by shooting. The same year, Williams was sentenced to death for four murders.

Williams spent 26 years on death row, before he was finally executed on December 13, 2005. In prison, he became an anti-gang activist, writing an autobiography, *Blue Rage, Black Redemption*, and eight children's books aimed at preventing young blacks joining gangs.

Hours before his death by lethal injection, Williams gave an interview to the Pacifica Radio station, in which he said, "I have been a wretched person, but I have redeemed myself. And I say to you and all those who can listen and will listen that redemption is tailor-made for the wretched, and that's what I used to be."

Today's Crips membership stands at around 60–65,000, made up of various gang sets such as the Asian Boyz and the Grape Street Watts Crips.

ACRONYMS: N

NCIS: National Criminal Intelligence Service. Established in 1992 this UK policing agency merged into the Serious Organized Crime Agency (SOCA) in 2006.

— STRANGE WAYS OF SMUGGLING DRUGS —

SWALLOWING

The commonest method of smuggling cocaine is by swallowing stuffed condoms or plastic bags. On arrival, drug mules take a laxative to pass the packets. The chief danger is of the packets bursting on the journey, with fatal results.

CLOTHING

Cocaine is often smuggled in the hollowed out soles of shoes or other items of clothing. In January 2008, a British woman was arrested wearing a padded bra filled with £50,000 worth of the drug. The *Daily Mail* dubbed this "The Plunderbra."

BEETLES

In 2007, customs officials in the Netherlands seized a shipment of 100 dead beetles, from Peru, which contained 300 grams of cocaine. Each beetle had been cut open, stuffed with the white powder, and then sewn back together again.

PUPPIES

In 2006, the US DEA broke up a Columbian heroin smuggling ring, whose method was to surgically implant bags of the liquid drug in the bellies of live puppies.

BROKEN LEG

In Barcelona airport, in 2009, a Chilean man was arrested after it was discovered that the cast on his broken left leg was made from cocaine. He was also carrying cocaine in his luggage and in a six-pack of beer.

SUITCASES

An Argentine woman was arrested in Santiago Airport, Chile, in 2009, as she was found carrying two suitcases made of cocaine mixed with resin. She aroused suspicion because her suitcases were heavier than their contents.

JESUS STATUE

In 2008, customs officials in Texas arrested a Mexican woman, who had a statue of Jesus, made of plaster mixed with cocaine, in the trunk of her car.

AFRICAN MASKS

In 2010, Canadian border officials stopped a 19-crate shipment of wooden masks and statues from Africa in order to check for insect pests. The objects were discovered to contain an impressive 1.7 tons of hashish.

"The man who has a conscience suffers whilst acknowledging his sin. That is his punishment."

FYODOR DOSTOYEVSKY (1821–1881), *Crime and Punishment*

— DR. JOHN BODKIN ADAMS (1899-1983) —

EASTBOURNE'S DR. ADAMS FIRST CAME under suspicion after he started inheriting large sums of money, following the deaths of his wealthy, elderly patients. When arrested on suspicion of murder on December 19, 1956, he replied, "Murder . . . murder . . . Can you prove it was murder? I didn't think you could prove it was murder. She was dying in any event." Despite a lengthy police investigation and the "Murder Trial of the Century," Adams was acquitted following the disappearance of valuable evidence and was never convicted. A subsequent trial did convict him of prescription fraud, lying on cremation forms, and failure to keep a dangerous drugs register. He was struck off the Medical Register but reinstated in 1961. He fell and broke his hip while shooting in 1983, and died in hospital after developing a chest infection. After his files were reopened in 2003 it is now believed that over his 30-year medical career Adams might have killed 160 of his own patients.

MARCEL PETIOT (1897-1946)

SERVING IN THE FRENCH ARMY before being gassed and diagnosed with mental illness during the First World War, Petiot retrained as a doctor. He became the mayor of Villeneuve-sur-Yonne and was elected as a councilor of the Yonne Department. He then moved to Paris. During the Second World War he ran an underground escape route for Jews and resistance fighters fleeing the Nazis. He promised them safe passage to South America in exchange for 25,000 Francs, but instead he would poison them with cyanide injections. Avoiding the Gestapo, Petiot survived the war and took part in the liberation of Paris, but was finally caught and arrested in 1944 after the remains of 23 people were found in his Paris home. He was suspected of having killed approximately 60 victims, although the exact number remains unknown. He was charged with 135 criminal charges and was finally convicted of 26 counts of murder. On May 25, 1946, Petiot was executed by guillotine.

POPULAR POISONS

BETWEEN 1750 AND 1914, the commonest poison used by murderers was arsenic. Out of 504 English criminal poisoning cases in the period, 237 involved arsenic. Arsenic was widely available, for it was used to control vermin, as a pesticide, and taken, in small doses, as a tonic. It was the perfect murder weapon because the symptoms of arsenic poisoning, vomiting and diarrhoea, were easy to mistake for those caused by dysentery and cholera.

Opium, often in the form of laudanum, was the second most popular, with 52 cases. The widespread use of opium meant that the symptoms of poisoning were easy for doctors to recognize. These were a slow pulse, flushed face, narrowing of the pupils and noisy breathing. Opium also left a distinctive odor around the deathbed, which one trial witness, in 1857, described as a "wild fierce smell." For the police, the difficulty lay in proving that an opium death was due to murder rather than an accident or suicide.

After opium came strychnine, with 41 cases. Strychnine, derived

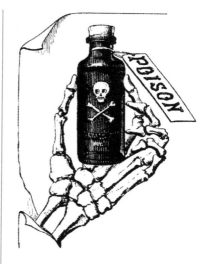

from the southeast Asian *nux vomica* plant, caused the most dramatic symptoms. Victims suffered violent convulsions before dying, in under an hour, from heart failure or asphyxiation. Strychnine was commonly available as a rat poison. It was favoured by the medical serial killers, Dr. William Palmer and Dr. Thomas Neil Cream.

ACRONYMS: O

OCCB: Organized Crime Control Bureau, charged with the investigation and prevention of organized crime in the US.
OIC: Officer In Charge or SOCO: Scene of Crime Officer.

CAMORRA

ITALY'S MOST RUTHLESS AND VIOLENT organized crime group is the Neapolitan Camorra, which has killed more people than either the Sicilian Mafia or the Calabrian 'Ndrangheta. The name Camorra, a blend of *capo* (boss) and *morra*, a hand game, is not used by Neapolitans, who prefer "Il Systema" (the system). Unlike the Mafia, with its pyramid structure, topped by a single boss, the Camorra is made up of over a hundred competing clans, each controlling a small area of Naples. Total membership is estimated at 6,700.

The clans are major importers of heroin from Asia, working with the Albanian Mafia and Nigerian drug gangs. In the 1990s, they moved into waste disposal, using southern Italy as an illegal dumping ground for toxic waste from the industrialized north. Yet another profitable business is counterfeit designer fashion, with fake Versace and Valentino clothing imported from China and manufactured in workshops in the outskirts of Naples.

In 2006, the Neapolitan journalist Roberto Saviano published *Gomorrah*, a chilling investigation into the system, later made into a film. Saviano, who saw his first murder at the age of 14, gathered information by working undercover in Camorra-controlled factories and construction sites. At the end of the book, he writes: "I was born in the land of the Camorra, in the territory with the most homicides in Europe, where savagery is interwoven with commerce, where nothing has value except what generates power." Saviano's book outraged the gangsters, who put a contract on his head. After spending two years under police protection, Saviano left Italy, and now lives in a secret location abroad.

SONGS OF THE CAMORRA

IN WORKING CLASS areas of Naples, one of the most popular forms of music is called "neomelodic," a mixture of Latin American, techno, pop, and traditional Neapolitan songs. What is unusual about the neo-melodic singers is that they are often ex-criminals, who sing songs that celebrate organized crime.

A typical song is *O Capo Clan* by Nello Liberti, with lyrics praising a Camorra boss. The video, which features real gangsters, shows a mob boss ordering a hit. Liberti, dressed in a white shell suit with gold jewelry, sings, "He's a serious man, it's not true he is evil . . . He respects us and we must respect him."

The term "neomelodic" was invented by an Italian journalist Federico Vacalebre, who told *Vice* magazine in 2009, "If gangster rap is the CNN of the American ghetto, neomelodics are the CNN of the Neapolitan ghetto . . . While the criminality of American gangster rap is more of a myth than anything else, our criminality is in fact very real and very scary."

I FOUGHT THE LAW

THE SOCIAL HISTORIAN HENRY MAYHEW described—in *London Labour and the London Poor* (1851)—the hatred of London's costermongers for the police:

"To serve out a policeman is the bravest act by which a coster-monger can distinguish himself. Some lads have been imprisoned upwards of a dozen times for this offence; and are consequently looked upon by their companions as martyrs. When they leave prison for such an act, a subscription is often got up for their benefit. In their continual warfare with the force, they resemble many savage nations, from the cunning and treachery they use. The lads endeavour to take the unsuspecting 'crusher' by surprise, and often crouch at the entrance of a court until a policeman passes, when a stone or a brick is hurled at him, and the youngster immediately disappears. Their love of revenge too, is extreme—their hatred being in no way mitigated by time; they will wait for months, following a policeman who has offended or wronged them, anxiously looking out for an opportunity of paying back the injury. One boy, I was told, vowed vengeance against a member of the force, and for six months never allowed the man to escape his notice. At length, one night, he saw the policeman in a row outside a public-house, and running into the crowd kicked him savagely, shouting at the same time: 'Now, you b-, I've got you at last.' When the boy heard that his persecutor was injured for life, his joy was very great, and he declared the twelve month's imprisonment he was sentenced to for the offence to be 'dirt cheap.'"

ACRONYMS: P

PC: Probable Cause to detain or arrest. Or in the UK, Police Constable.
PO: Probation or parole officer.
PD: Police Department. This suffix goes after every city and town's name, i.e. San Francisco Police Department is abbreviated to SFPD.

IAN BRADY (1938-)

TOGETHER WITH HIS GIRLFRIEND Myra Hindley, Ian Brady abducted, sexually assaulted, and murdered five young people and children between July 1963 and October 1965. Hindley would be convicted of two of the murders. Most of their victims were buried on the Yorkshire Moors and to this day the grave of Brady's third victim, 12-year-old Keith Bennett, has never been discovered. The death penalty in the United Kingdom was abolished one month before the arrest of Brady and Hindley. He was sentenced to three counts life imprisonment, with no possibility of parole, and after being diagnosed as a psychopath in 1985, currently resides in the Ashworth Psychiatric Hospital in Sefton.

———RUSSAN CRIMINAL TATTOOS———

DANZIG BALDAYEV (BORN 1925) WAS A Russian prison guard who, in 1948, began to collect prisoners' tattoos. Over 50 years, he drew and photographed around 3,600 tattoos, which he published in a three-volume encyclopedia. Launching the first volume in 2001, Baldayev said, "To my mind, tattoos are the media of the prisons, a unique language of symbols."

This is a list of some of the tattoos, and their meanings:

BARBED WIRE: each spike represents one year of imprisonment

CAT: the sign of the thief. A single cat means the thief worked alone; several cats mean that he belonged to a gang

COBWEBS: often tattooed on the shoulders, the sign of a drug addict

DAGGER THROUGH THE NECK: reveals that the wearer has killed in prison, and will kill again for a fee. The number of drops of blood show the number of killings

MILITARY EPAULETTES ON THE SHOULDERS: sign of a high-ranking criminal

GENIE COMING OUT OF A LAMP: the inmate is serving time for drug-related crimes or is a drug addict

KNIGHT IN ARMOR: indicates a violent sadist

PRISON BARS: an inmate with a life sentence

ROSE WITH THORNS: someone who went to prison as a teenager

SKULLS: worn by murderers and high-ranking criminals

STARS ON THE KNEES: the inmate refuses to kneel for any authority

> *"If you ever have occasion to chop a body up in the bath, never saw the arms off first, otherwise the torso will keep spinning as you cut the rest. It makes it awkward."*
>
> *Grendon Underwood prison inmate in*
> *A Rusty Gun: Facing Up to a Life of Crime, 2010*
> BY FORMER ARMED ROBBER, NOEL "RAZOR" SMITH

YAKUZA

THE WORLD'S LARGEST criminal organization is the Yakuza of Japan. Today there are thought to be more than 87,000 Yakuza members—four times as many as belong to the US Mafia.

The Yakuza rose to power after World War Two, when Japan was occupied by the US military, and there were huge profits to be made on the black market. The name Yakuza is derived from the losing hand in a card game, with three cards numbered ya (8) ku (9) and za (3). The name is the Yakuza way of identifying themselves as "losers," outside normal society.

Though their wealth mostly comes from gambling, drugs, prostitution, and extortion, the Yakuza are regarded as semi-legal. They have a public profile, with offices listed in phone books. The largest syndicate, the Yamaguchi-gumi, based in Kobe, resembles a big corporation. They even have their own fan magazines. After the 1995 Kobe earthquake and the 2011 tsunami, the Yamaguchi-gumi provided emergency relief, sending truckloads of supplies to the stricken disaster areas. In the Yakuza, as in the rest of Japanese culture, there is a strong emphasis on loyalty and respect for seniors. Membership is based on the relationship between an *oyabun* (father) and *kobun* (foster child). Recruits are "adopted" by an oyabun in a ceremony in which they share a cup of sake. Members are called *teppodama*, or bullets, to be fired by their boss.

Those who offend their bosses have to atone with a ritual called *yobitsume* (finger shortening). The offender cuts off the end joint of his little finger, which he then graciously offers to his boss wrapped in cloth. With each further offence, another joint must be cut off.

Many members have full body tattoos, painfully applied with bamboo needles. Young members, called *chimpira*, wear luridly colored sports clothes and favor a tight "punch perm" hairstyle.

The Yakuza wield considerable political power in Japan, through extreme right-wing nationalist groups known as *uyoku dantai*. Despite recent laws to prevent Yakuza doing business they remain integral in Japanese society.

ACRONYMS: Q

QPM: Queen's Police Medal for Distinguished Service, for gallantry or distinguished service. Created in 1954.

CARYL WHITTIER CHESSMAN (1921-1960)

CHESSMAN WAS A CAREER criminal who spent most of his adult life behind bars. He had recently been paroled when he was arrested near Los Angeles and charged with being the notorious "Red Light Bandit." He allegedly followed people in their cars to secluded areas and flashed a red light that tricked them into thinking he was a police officer. He would rob them and, in several young women's cases, rape them. At the time, under California law, any crime that involved kidnapping with bodily harm was considered a capital offense. Chessman vigorously

asserted his innocence, saying he was both the victim of mistaken identity and a much larger conspiracy framing him. He claimed to know who the real culprit was, but refused to name him. In July 1948, Chessman was convicted on 17 counts of robbery, kidnapping, and rape, and was condemned to death. Chessman argued his case in public, through letters, essays, and four books, igniting a worldwide movement to spare his life. California Governor Pat Brown was flooded with appeals for clemency from noted authors including Aldous Huxley, Ray Bradbury, Norman Mailer, and Robert Frost, and former First Lady Eleanor Roosevelt.

Over the 11 years and 10 months he spent on death row—the longest on record at the time—Chessman successfully avoided eight execution deadlines, often by hours. Governor Brown issued a last minute, 60-day stay of execution on February 19, 1960, but this ran out in April and Chessman finally went to the gas chamber on May 2, 1960. As the execution began, and the chamber filled with gas, the telephone rang. It was a judge's secretary informing the warden of a new stay of execution. The warden replied, "It's too late; the execution has begun." The secretary had initially misdialed the number.

BARCELONA PICKPOCKETS

BARCELONA IN SPAIN is famous for its skilled pickpockets, who target vulnerable tourists for their wallets, handbags, cameras, and phones. Thieves operate in teams, in which some create a distraction, while another will steal, and yet another will make the getaway.

In 2012, Chris Rogers of the BBC interviewed Johnny, Mario, and Danny, three Romanian pickpockets in Barcelona, who offered to demonstrate their methods. "They demonstrate a tactic named after Ronaldinho, the footballer who dances when he scores. Johnny approaches with a map, asking for directions, while Mario and Danny pretend to be drunk, swinging their arms and forcing me to dance. They run off in different directions and Danny returns, proudly holding my wallet. I didn't notice a thing, it all happened so quickly. 'I am the distracter,' explains Johnny. 'Mario is the pickpocket or the distracter because he is very experienced, and if he takes your wallet or phone, he hands it to Danny; he is the runner. That way the tourist has no idea who did it or who has their belongings.'"

THIEVES IN THE GULAG

ONE OF THE LARGEST PENAL systems in history was the Soviet Gulag, an acronym standing for "Chief Administration of Corrective Labor Camps." This was a network of penal labor camps, stretching for 6,000 miles across the former USSR. Established by Joseph Stalin in 1930, the camps steadily expanded until, by the time of his death in 1953, their population had risen to 1,727,970 prisoners.

Life in the Gulag is well documented, thanks to the memoirs of Alexander Solzhenitsyn, John Noble, and other prisoners. A major theme of these memoirs is the division between the political prisoners, who formed the majority in the camps, and the violent professional criminals (*blatnois*) who preyed upon them. The criminals belonged to a separate society, whose members called themselves the *vory v zakone*, or "thieves in law." They followed their own code, whose first rule was that they did not cooperate with the authorities. Their refusal to work was tolerated by the camp authorities, who used them to control the other inmates. As John Noble recalled in his 1959 book, *I Was a Slave in Russia*, "Our camp was ruled with a steel fist by about 250 blatnois, the Russian criminals. They kept the political prisoners in abject fear . . . They spent their time sleeping, stealing whatever they admired, sharpening the knives they made, playing home-made balalaikas, dancing the plashka, a fast dance something like Spanish Flamenco . . . If one of them should so much as lift a shovel, he would be murdered instantly by his companions."

ACRONYMS: R

RAP: Record of Arrests and Prosecutions. Any recidivist's criminal record, otherwise know as a "Rap sheet."
RCMP: Royal Canadian Mounted Police, colloquially known as "The Mounties."

—— DOROTHEA PUENTE (1929-2011) ——

PUENTE RAN A FOUR-BEDROOM boarding house in Sacramento, California, and is believed by investigators to have murdered nine of her guests, most of them elderly. She would poison them and continue to cash social security checks. The bodies of seven people were discovered buried in her yard in 1988, and the 59-year-old was arrested. For the rest of her life she maintained her innocence and insisted all her tenants had died of natural causes. Convicted of three murders and sentenced to life imprisonment without parole, she finally died in prison, aged 82.

SAFE CRACKING

NEXT TO BURGLARY, THE ASSOCIATED art of breaking into a safe is possibly the only other crime that has been truly romanticized by contemporary fiction, with characters like Raffles in *The Amateur Cracksman* (1899) and films such as *Die Hard* (1988). Some of the earliest strong boxes were invented by British locksmiths Charles and Jeremiah Chubb, back in 1835. Since then, thieves have been looking at ways of breaking into safes. Early methods were crude, involving heavy hammers, chisels, and dynamite, which risked damaging the contents.

Then, in the late 1800s, expert cracksman Langdon W. Morse developed a new technique of drilling a small hole near the handle of a vault door, pouring in blasting powder, and covering the spot with a blanket or rug and lighting the fuse.

When liquid nitroglycerin was invented, it was quickly adopted. The *Ashburton Guardian* described the process on September 8, 1919, "The skilled cracksman makes his own gelignite and carries it, if he is a careful man, in an India-rubber hot-water bottle; a careless operator may carry it in an ordinary glass bottle. It is technically known as 'the soup' or 'the oil.'" The New Zealand newspaper continued, " . . . the 'inside' men, breaking in, proceed to seal up the cracks of the safe door with common washing soap, well softened, leaving a slight aperture unsealed at the top of the door. Round this a soap dam is built into which the soup is poured. The liquid quickly finds its way about the cracks of the safe, and in a few moments it is ready to be exploded. This is done by means of a fuse and detonator. A single shot will sometimes demolish a door. If it does not, another charge is made. To pocket the contents of a safe is a matter of moments. A good motor car will do the rest."

THE SAFEST PLACES ON EARTH?

BELOW ARE COUNTRIES WITH THE lowest murder rates in the world, based on reported cases in the 2011 report from United Nations Office on Drugs and Crime:

1. Anguilla	1	6. Guam	1
2. Liechtenstein	1	7. French Polynesia	1
3. Andorra	1	8. Iceland	1
4. Tonga	1	9. Monaco	0
5. Federated States of Micronesia	1	10. Palau	0

PABLO ESCOBAR

PABLO ESCOBAR WAS A Columbian drug lord, shot dead by the police on December 2, 1993. At the height of his power, he had ordered the assassinations of judges, police officers, and many rivals. He was also responsible for the bombing of Avianca Airlines Flight 203, in 1989, in which 110 people were killed. At the same time, he cultivated a Robin Hood image, giving money to the poor, and building hospitals, schools, and churches. Escobar was so popular with poor Columbians that 20,000 people attended his funeral.

In 1992, the US Joint Special Operations command began a manhunt for Escobar, training a Columbian task force, called the Search Bloc. On the last day of his life, knowing the Search Bloc was closing in, he wrote a letter to imprisoned drug lord Carlos Ledher, in Florida: "Sometimes I do feel that I did go too far with the kidnappings and the bombings, especially because as a consequence my little girl has had to grow up under constant persecution; and though I can understand that the deaths of all those people antagonized the country against me, you understand why it had to be done. The stupid and corrupt government, had to be made to understand that I was serious about not allowing myself be handed over the gringos . . . I will never be forced to leave my country while I'm alive, as I have said, I prefer to be in a grave in Colombia than in a jail cell in the United States."

FOOL'S GOLD

ONE OF THE MOST SUCCESSFUL, and brutal, robberies of all time took place on November 26, 1983. Six men broke into the Brink's-MAT warehouse at Heathrow Airport expecting to steal £3 million ($4.5 million) in cash. What they discovered, and stole, was £26 million ($39 million)—the equivalent of £100 million ($151 million) in today's money—in gold, diamonds, and cash. They gained access thanks to their inside security man, Antony Black, who was the brother-in-law of one of the thieves, Brian Robson. The savage gang poured petrol over the staff and threatened to set fire to them if they didn't provide the combinations to the vault. The heist was described, at the time, as "The crime of the century" and most of the three tones of gold were never recovered. Black, Robson, and Micky McAvoy all served time, but the remaining four robbers were never convicted. However there was no honor amongst thieves, and "the curse of Brinks-MAT" led to five related shootings in the three years after the raid. The gold bullion launderer Kenneth Noye ended up serving a life sentence for an unrelated murder, after becoming "Britain's most wanted man" having stabbed Stephen Cameron to death in an alleged "road rage" incident.

— FIVE MOVIES BASED ON REAL CRIMINALS —

HENRY, PORTRAIT OF A SERIAL KILLER (1986) dir. John McNaughton
Based of the life of Henry Lee Lucas, who murdered at least 11 people (possibly hundreds) between 1960 and 1983, this controversial low-budget film disturbed many audiences, as it became a cult video hit.

BADLANDS (1973) dir. Terrence Malick
Starring Martin Sheen as Kit and Sissy Spacek as Holly, this movie fictionalized the Charles Starkweather/Caril Fugate 1958 murder spree. As Fugate was still alive at the time, the filmmakers changed the names to avoid a lawsuit.

10 RILLINGTON PLACE (1971) dir. Richard Fleischer
Sir Richard Attenborough played British serial killer John Christie, who killed at least eight women at the London address. The film also focuses on Timothy Evans who was hanged for the murders of his wife and daughter, when it was, in fact, Christie who was responsible. Attenborough commented in *The Times*, "It is a most devastating statement on capital punishment."

BUSTER (1988) dir. David Green
This comedy/drama starred Phil Collins as Buster Edwards, who took part in The Great Train Robbery of 1963. Edwards went on the run but returned to serve nine years in prison. Once released, he was found hanging from a steel girder in 1994. The inquest gave an open verdict to whether it was suicide.

ROPE (1948) dir. Alfred Hitchcock
Inspired by the murder of 14-year-old Bobby Franks in 1924 by two rich university students, Nathan Leopold and Richard Loeb. Leopold and Loeb, wanted to commit the "perfect crime" but were caught and sentenced to life.

———————————— ACRONYMS: S ————————————

SOCA: Serious Organized Crime Agency. Division of the British police set up to act as a single point of contact for international enquiries and all UK police and law enforcement agencies.
SWAT: Special Weapons And Tactics. Name for US law enforcement units, which use military-style light weapons and specialized tactics in high-risk operations that fall outside of the abilities of regular, uniformed police.

———— PSST…WANNA BUY A TOWER? ————

BOHEMIAN VICTOR LUSTIG WAS A confidence trickster who started off small, with the classic $100 bill scam. He would show people in Paris a device that could print $100 bills. The only problem, he explained, is that it only prints one bill every six hours. Many people paid him enormous amounts of money (often in excess of $30,000) for the device. In reality, the device contained only two real $100 bills. Once they were "printed" out by the machine it would produce only blank paper. By the time the marks realized, Lustig was long gone, with a 12-hour head start with their cash.

But Lustig soon moved onto more ambitious cons. In 1925, France was recovering from World War One, and the upkeep of the Eiffel Tower was a huge expense for Paris. Lustig read about this and came up with his most brilliant idea. After forging government documents, he invited six scrap metal dealers to a secret meeting in a hotel. He revealed that the city could not afford to keep the tower and that they were going to sell it for scrap. He swore them all to secrecy to avoid the public becoming distressed at the idea of the losing the tower.

The Eiffel Tower was meant to be only temporary and Lustig's scam was just 18 years after it was supposed to have been taken down, so it all seemed plausible. Lustig took the dealers in a limousine to tour the tower, and one of the dealers, Andre Poisson, was so convinced that the tale was legitimate he handed over the money. When he realized he had been conned, he was too embarrassed to tell the police and Lustig escaped with the cash. A month later, Lustig returned to Paris to try the whole scam again. However, this time it was reported to the police, and Lustig had to make a speedy escape.

Setting up base in the USA, Lustig even convinced notorious Chicago gangster Al Capone to invest $50,000. He stored the money in a vault and returned it two months later, stating that the deal had fallen through. Capone—so impressed by Lustig's "honesty"—gave him $5,000 for his effort. In 1934, Lustig was found guilty of counterfeiting, pleaded guilty, and was sentenced to 20 years in Alcatraz. He died of pneumonia in 1947 while still incarcerated in a Springfield, Missouri jail, an ignominious end for "The Man who Sold the Eiffel Tower."

———— ACRONYMS: T ————

TCD: Traffic Control Division.
TFU: Tactical Firearms Unit. British police department with the capability to deal with armed criminals.

ALBERTO DESALVO (1931-1973)

"THE BOSTON STRANGLER" terrorized the city's women between 1962 and 1964. In 1967, Alberto DeSalvo was arrested and convicted of rape and burglary, and subsequently confessed to being The Strangler. He was sentenced to life imprisonment. Despite his confession, grave doubts now exist as to whether or not DeSalvo was actually responsible for the 13 victims he claimed. Some believed he confessed to help raise money for his wife and child. Later, fellow inmate George Nassar, to whom DeSalvo had allegedly confessed, claimed responsibility for some of the murders, but recanted this in a 1999 interview with the *Boston Globe*. Certain experts noted that the modus operandi varied in each attack and that forensic evidence did not match DeSalvo's story. He was stabbed to death in prison.

—————————— THE BLACK MUSEUM ——————————

I N 1869 THE PRISONERS PROPERTY ACT was passed, which allowed the British authorities to collect prisoners' possessions, with the aim of helping the police further their criminological studies. By 1874 the collection had been expanded considerably by founders Inspector Neame and P.C. Randall, and the following year it was turned into an official, but private, museum.

The first official visitors were Police Commissioner Sir Edmund Henderson and Assistant Commissioners Lt. Col. Labolmondiere and Capt. Harris, along with other dignitaries, on October 6, 1877. *The Observer* newspaper, somewhat bitterly, gave the exhibition its grim moniker that same year, after a reporter was denied access by Neame.

Inspired by the museum, radio producer Harry Towers launched a 1951 radio series, hosted by Orson Welles, called *The Black Museum*. Each week the show focused on a different object from the museum and a recreated a grisly story relating to the artifact.

Officially known as The Crime Museum, the exhibit has been moved to several locations its 140-year history, including the Metropolitan Police Offices in 1890 and then to New Scotland Yard in the Eighties, where it is currently located at the suitably titled, Room 101.

Today, the museum consists of two rooms, the first being a reconstruction of the original museum, with a large collection of murder weapons. Alongside these are other morbid curiosities such as a variety of criminals' death masks and hangman's nooses, including the ones used to execute Peter Allen and Gwynne Evans, the UK's last-ever executions. There is also the infamous, "From Hell" letter allegedly written by Jack the Ripper. The second room contains cabinets relating to Famous Murders, Notorious Poisoners, Murder of Police Officers, Royalty, Bank Robberies, Espionage, Sieges, and Hostages and Hijacking.

The museum holds over 500 crime-related items including the world's most prolific forger Charles Black's set of printing plates, forged banknotes, and a hollowed-out kitchen door used to hide them. Other items include a fake De Beers diamond from the Millennium Dome heist in 2000, and British serial killer Dennis Nilsen's actual stove, on which he boiled down his victims' body parts.

While the Crime Museum remains closed to the public, it has been visited by a wide range of luminaries including authors Sir Arthur Conan Doyle and Jerome K. Jerome, Harry Houdini, Stan Laurel and Oliver Hardy, and various members of the Royal Family, such as The Prince of Wales (later to be Edward VII).

The museum is currently used as a lecture theatre on topics such as Forensic Science, Pathology, Law, and Investigative Techniques.

KNOW YOUR MURDERS

AMICICIDE: killing a friend

ANDROCIDE: the systematic killing of men

AUTOCIDE: suicide by crashing a car

DOMINICIDE: the act of killing one's master

ECOCIDE: the destruction of the natural environment by such activity as war, overexploitation of resources, or pollution

EPISCOPICIDE: the act of killing a bishop

FAMILICIDE: is a multiple homicide where the killer's spouse and children are slain

FEMICIDE (also Gynaecide): the systematic killing of women

FILICIDE: the act of a parent killing his or her son or daughter

FRATRICIDE: the act of killing a brother, or the military term for death by friendly fire

GENOCIDE: the systematic extermination of an entire national, racial, religious, or ethnic group

GERONTICIDE: the act of killing the elderly, or abandoning them to die, or commit suicide

HOMICIDE: the intentional act of killing of another human being

INFANTICIDE: the intentional act of killing a young child

MARITICIDE: the act of killing one's husband

MATRICIDE: the murder of one's mother

MEDICIDE: a suicide achieved with the aid of a doctor

NEONATICIDE: killing an infant within the first 24 hours of its life

OMNICIDE: the unintentional act of killing all humans, for example by global nuclear war

PATRICIDE: the act of killing of one's father

POPULICIDE: the slaughter of the people

REGICIDE: the murder of a king

SORORICIDE: the murder of one's sister

SUICIDE: intentional killing of self

TYRANNICIDE: killing a tyrant

UXORICIDE: the act of killing one's wife

VATICIDE: the act of killing a prophet

ACRONYMS: U

USDSA: United States Deputy Sheriffs Association.

TOM CLINCH

JONATHAN SWIFT, AUTHOR OF *Gulliver's Travels*, wrote the poem *Clever Tom Clinch Going to Be Hanged*, in 1727:

As clever Tom Clinch, while the rabble was bawling,
Rode stately through Holborn to die in his calling,
He stopped at the "George" for a bottle of sack,
And promised to pay for it—when he came back.
His waistcoat, and stockings, and breeches were white,
His cap had a new cherry-ribbon to tie't;
And the maids to the doors and the balconies ran,
And cried "Lack-a-day! he's a proper young man!"
But, as from the windows the ladies he spy'd,
Like a beau in the box, he bow'd low on each side;
And when his last speech the loud hawkers did cry,
He swore from his cart, it was all a damn'd lye.
The hangman for pardon fell down on his knee;
Tom gave him a kick in the guts for his fee.
Then said, I must speak to the people a little,
But I'll see you all damn'd before I will whittle.
My honest friend wild, may he long hold his place,
He lengthen'd my life with a whole year of grace.
Take courage, dear comrades, and be not afraid,
Nor slip this occasion to follow your trade.
My conscience is clear, and my spirits are calm,
And thus I go off without pray'r-book or psalm.
Then follow the practice of clever Tom Clinch,
Who hung like a hero, and never would flinch.

"When you're young and strong and you can afford to throw away a decade or two in some pisshole prison and still have plenty of life left to live, it's all a big laugh. Then you wake up one morning and see a strange face staring back at you from the shaving mirror. Some old geezer with bitter, weary eyes where there used to be a devil-may-care twinkle."

NOEL "RAZOR" SMITH
A Rusty Gun: Facing Up to a Life of Crime, 2010

> *"He who has never tasted jail,*
> *Lives well within the legal pale,*
> *While he who's served a heavy sentence,*
> *Renews the racket, not repentance."*
>
> OGDEN NASH (1902–1971), *I'm a Stranger Here Myself*

CANNIBAL CLAN

THE MOST LURID BIOGRAPHY IN *The Newgate Calendar* is that of Alexander "Sawney" Beane, the Scottish cannibal. In the late 16th century, Beane and his wife lived in a cave on the coast of south-west Scotland. They were robbers, who killed and ate their victims. Over 25 years, the Beanes had eight sons, six daughters, eighteen grandsons, and fourteen granddaughters—products of incest.

The cannibals escaped detection until they ambushed a couple riding home from a fair. While the wife was seized and butchered, her husband escaped to raise the alarm. A few days later, a posse with bloodhounds discovered Beane's cave, which was filled with human limbs, some hanging up like dried beef, others soaked in pickle.

The Beanes were taken to Edinburgh and executed without trial. The menfolk had their "privy members," hands, and legs chopped off, and were left to bleed to death. Then the women were thrown into three separate fires, where they died cursing the watching crowd.

According to *The Newgate Calendar*, the story of the Beanes would be rejected as incredible were it not supported "by the most unquestionable historical evidence." Yet there is no record of the Beanes in any contemporary Scottish source. The story, which presents Scots as savages, is thought to be an English invention. It dates from the early 1700s, when there was strong anti-Scottish sentiment in England, due to the Jacobite uprisings.

Another earlier, lesser-known, Scottish cannibal legend is that of Christie-Cleek (AKA Andrew Christie), a Perth butcher who allegedly hacked up 30 victims during a famine in the mid-14th century and fed them to his starving group. The veracity of this story is equally dubious and Christie-Cleek quickly became a boogeyman to scare Scottish children.

Despite its English origins, the story of Sawney Beane has been embraced in Scotland. Today, tourists are directed to Sawney Beane's cave at Bennane Head in South Ayrshire. The Edinburgh Dungeon tourist attraction has a replica of the cave, with the grisly leftovers of lost travelers. Visitors are asked, "Will you escape or become the cannibal's next fresh meat?"

FRANK COSTELLO (1891-1973)

STARTING OFF with bootlegging, gambling, and slot machines, Mafioso Costello (real name: Francesco Castiglia) slowly worked his way up the ladder to become the boss of the Luciano crime family in 1937. Despite being the head of the biggest crime organization in American history, he was never convicted of murder or of violent assault, and in fact claimed he never carried a gun. However, Costello was convicted of contempt of Senate charges in August 1952 after walking out of the Kefauver hearings, and went to jail for 18 months. Released after 14 months, Costello was then charged with tax evasion in 1954 and sentenced to five years imprisonment. Costello served 11 months, before it was overturned on appeal. In 1956 he was convicted again, but released in early 1957 after another successful appeal. He survived an assassination attempt in 1957 after Vito Genovese, planning to take over the family, contracted a hit. The "Prime Minister of the Underworld" eventually died of a heart attack on February 18, 1973. He was partly the inspiration for the character of Vito Corleone in *The Godfather*.

—— CONFIDENCE TRICKSTERS' LEXICON ——

THE MARK: the intended victim of a planned con

SHORT CON: refers to taking The Mark for all the money he has on his person. It's an opportunist scam that isn't greatly pre-planned

A LONG, OR BIG, CON: a more complex, planned con, where The Mark is sent to get more money, or used to get more money than they have on them. The Big Con is a form of theatre—"staged with minute naturalistic illusionism for an audience of one who is enlisted as part of the cast"

PUTTING HIM ON THE SEND: another term for a long con

THE BIG STORE: there are two types of con settings, real life venues (e.g. restaurants and hotel rooms) and where empty offices are set up to look like the real deal, this latter is The Big Store

THE ROPER: The Outsideman who identifies with The Mark and gains their confidence

THE INSIDEMAN: the key player, who stays near The Big Store and receives The Mark who The Roper brings in

THE MANAGER: runs the outfit and is often the bookmaker for the group

EXTRAS: unemployed conmen playing the role of extras in the con

PUTTING UP THE MARK: the process of locating a wealthy victim or mark

PLAYING THE CON FOR HIM: refers to gaining the victim's confidence

ROPING THE MARK: is steering him to meet The Insideman who will eventually fleece him

GIVING HIM THE CONVINCER: the process of allowing the victim to make a substantial profit on the first scam, thereby gaining his trust

BLOWING HIM OFF: getting the victim out of the way as quickly as possible

PUTTING THE FIX: forestalling action by the Law

PLAYING A MAN AGAINST THE WALL: conning a victim in a real setting, e.g. a hotel room

CACKLE-BLADDER: faking the death of one of the conmen. It involves filling a small receptacle with chicken blood, which the con artist hides on their person and bursts for the fake gunshot

BEEFS: The Mark goes to the police to grass up the conmen

THE FIX: the cooperation bought from the police. A Fixer usually has political connections and is paid off by the conmen for fixing people in the banks, police, and the courts. Most con mobs can't exist without a good Fixer

ROBERT CHARLES

IN NEW ORLEANS, IN JULY 1900, a black newspaper seller called Robert Charles went on a shooting spree, killing 27 white people, including four policemen. The killings, which caused rioting across the city, were remembered by the jazz musician Jelly Roll Morton in his memoirs:

"Robert Charles sold newspapers on the corner of Dryad and Melpomeme . . . He never made any noise bigger than 'Get your Picayune, Get your paper!' until the day he had an argument with his wife and she called the police . . . Robert Charles was arrested and the policeman wouldn't let him go back after his hat. He was a very orderly seeming guy, but this aroused him to fury. He broke away, taken a Winchester rifle, killed the policeman and from that the riot started, in which all sorts of innocent people were killed . . . Well, if you shoot one officer like Robert Charles had, it's no more than right that another should take his place, but the way that newsboy was killing them off it looked like the department might run out of officers. Every time he raised his rifle and got a policeman in the sights, there'd be another one dead . . .

"Like many other bad men, he had a song originated on him. This song was squished very easily by the department . . . due to the fact that it was a trouble breeder . . . I once knew the Robert Charles song, but I found out it was best for me to forget it and that I did in order to go along with the world on the peaceful side."

ACRONYMS: V

VPS: Victim Personal Statement. Set up by the UK's Crown Prosecution Service to give victims the opportunity to state how the crime has affected them—physically, emotionally, psychologically, financially, or in any other way.

THE GARROTTING PANIC

IN JULY 1862, THE BRITISH MP Hugh Pilkington, on his way from Parliament to his club, was mugged by two men, who seized him around the throat and stole his watch. The newspapers claimed that this was part of a crime wave, and named this type of robbery "garrotting," after the Spanish method of execution by strangling.

In fact, there had been just as many violent robberies the previous year, but the robbing of an MP made garrotting stories newsworthy. This created a panic among the Victorian middle classes. While some people became too terrified to leave their homes in the evening, others formed "anti-garrotting societies" to hunt down garrotters. Several innocent men were mistakenly attacked or dragged to the police station.

The garrotting scare is an example of a "moral panic," a term popularized by the sociologist Stanley Cohen. In his 1972 book, *Moral Panics and Folk Devils*, Cohen wrote, "Societies appear to be subject, every now and then, to periods of moral panic. A condition, episode, person, or group of persons emerges to become defined as a threat to societal values and interests; its nature is presented in a stylized and stereotypical fashion by the mass media; the moral barricades are manned by editors, bishops, politicians, and other right thinking people; socially accredited experts pronounce their diagnoses and solutions."

The result of the garroting panic was that the government was pressurized into passing a "Garrotters Act," in 1863, which introduced flogging, on top of imprisonment, as a punishment for violent robbery.

CORLEONE APOLOGIZES

IN JANUARY 2013, THE MAYOR of Corleone held a ceremony marking the 10th anniversary of the arrest of the Mafia supreme boss, Totò Riina. Nick Squires in the *Daily Telegraph* reported: "Leoluchina Savona apologized to victims of the Mafia's vendettas, bombings, and killings on behalf of the inhabitants of the town, which was immortalized by *The Godfather* book and subsequent films starring Marlon Brando and Al Pacino. 'I apologize in the name of all the people of Corleone. I ask forgive-ness for the blood that was spilled,' the mayor said on Monday . . . 'To the Mafia, I ask you to leave this land, to abandon the struggle. I ask them to admit defeat, to surrender.'"

TED BUNDY (1946-1989)

WHILE NOT THE MOST PROLIFIC, Bundy is still one of the most notorious serial killers of all time. He raped and murdered his way across the USA for four years from 1974–1978, and when finally caught confessed to raping and murdering 30 victims, although at one time he claimed a number of over 100. Charismatic, handsome, and intelligent, he easily won his victims' trust, despite admitting he was ". . . the most cold-hearted son of a bitch you'll ever meet." Bundy's technique of wearing a fake arm plaster cast and luring some of his victims into his van was used as a plot device in the *Silence of the Lambs*. He was arrested and while on trial in 1977 escaped from the Courthouse in Aspen, Colorado, and was on the run for six days. Six months later he escaped again from jail, but was caught in Florida, two months later, after claiming more victims. The former law student defended himself in court, but was ultimately sentenced to death. He was executed by electric chair.

CAPITAL PUNISHMENT

WHILE MANY WESTERN COUNTRIES (currently 97) have now banned the death penalty, there are still many (including China, Japan, and the United States) that actively use it for crimes ranging from murder to drug smuggling. There are numerous ways that modern death sentences have been carried out:

LETHAL INJECTION

Despite originally being postulated by New York Dr. Julius Bleyer as a cheaper alternative to hanging back in January 17, 1888, it wasn't used as a form of execution for 94 years, when Charles Brooks, Jr. was injected in Texas on December 7, 1982. Chapman's Protocol (named after Oklahoma's state medical examiner, Jay Chapman) involves two intravenous lines (the second as a back-up) in which a series of drugs are given in order. The condemned is given three separate injections: Sodium thiopental or pentobarbital which renders the prisoner unconscious. This is followed by pancuronium bromide, a muscle relaxant, which causes paralysis of the respiratory muscles and would eventually cause asphyxiation. Finally, potassium chloride stops the heart, causing a fatal cardiac arrest.

ELECTRIC CHAIR

"Old Sparky" was invented as a replacement to hanging by Harold P. Brown and Arthur Kennelly, employees of Thomas Edison, and was first adopted in 1889. It's first victim was William Kemmler in New York's Auburn Prison on August 6, 1890. He had to be shocked twice, initially with 1,000 volts and the second time with 2,000 volts. It took eight minutes, with fellow electrical entrepreneur George Westinghouse commenting that "they would have done better using an axe."

HANGING

There are four ways of judicial hanging: the short drop, suspension hanging, the long drop, and the standard drop. The suspension provides a crude, long, slow death by asphyxiation, whereas the long drop technique is highly specialized. However, if done incorrectly, it can remove the condemned's head when the rope snaps tight. The botched hanging and subsequent decapitation of Eva Dugan in 1930 caused Arizona state to switch to the gas chamber.

GAS CHAMBER

Still used in California, Missouri, and Arizona, this technique involves the chamber filling with either hydrogen cyanide, carbon dioxide, or carbon monoxide. The first person in America to be executed this way was Gee Jon, on February 8, 1924.

FIRING SQUAD

This is the most common form of execution globally, with 70 countries using this method. There are many forms, from a shot to the back of the head or neck from a mounted gun, to a firing squad of five, aiming at the heart, with one of the squad firing a blank "conscience round." North Korea is one of the few countries to still perform firing squad executions in public.

BEHEADING

This method has been mostly used, in modern times, in Arabic states like Qatar and Saudi Arabia, but it was a popular form of execution in France, via "Madame Guillotine," right up until 1977, when torture-murderer Hamida Djandoubi was the last person to be guillotined.

ACRONYMS: W

WPP: Witness Protection Program. Administered by the US Department of Justice, it provides new identities with authentic documentation and relocates witnesses under threat.

WHERE NOT TO GO ON HOLIDAY

ACCORDING TO THE UNITED NATIONS OFFICE on Drugs and Crime's 2011 report, the best place to avoid visiting is Honduras, which had a murder rate of 91.6 per 100,000 inhabitants or 7,104 deaths (up from 82.1 or 6,239 murders, the previous year). Here's a run down of the top ten highest murder rates in the world:

1. Brazil	40,974		**6.** Nigeria	18,422
2. India	40,752		**7.** South Africa	15,940
3. Mexico	25,757		**8.** Russia	14,574
4. Ethopia	20,239		**9.** Columbia	13,863
5. Indonesia	18,963		**10.** Pakistan	13,860

In comparison, the United States of America had 12,996 (4.2 per 100,000) and the United Kingdom had 722 murders (1.2 per 100,000) putting them 14th and 73rd, respectively, on the list.

DANIEL LEE SIEBERT (1954-2008)

SERIAL KILLER SIEBERT STRANGLED FOUR people, although he confessed to five murders in Alabama and hinted that he was responsible for at least a dozen more. He first caught the authorities attention in 1979 when he served time for manslaughter. Then in 1986, he murdered two students from the Alabama Institute for the Deaf and Blind in Talladega, Linda Jarman and Sherri Weathers, and the latter's two children. He was convicted of three of the murders and was sentenced to death. After spending 21 years on death row he died following complications due to pancreatic cancer, just one day before his execution by lethal injection.

——— SIX GREAT CON ARTIST FILMS ———

THE GRIFTERS (1990) dir. Stephen Frears
Based on a Jim Thompson novel, small-time con man Roy Dillon (John Cusack) is torn between loyalty to his mother, Lily (Angelica Huston), and new girlfriend, Myra Langtry (Annette Bening), as they attempt to pull "The Rag" scam. Like all good con movies, you never know who's conning who until the final reel.

THE STING (1973) dir. George Roy Hill
In 1930s Chicago, an inexperienced grifter, Johnny Hooker (Robert Redford), teams up with old hand Henry Gondorff (Paul Newman), to take a criminal banker, Doyle Lonnegan (Robert Shaw), for the "Big Con" in revenge for their friend's murder.

DIRTY ROTTEN SCOUNDRELS (1988) dir. Frank Oz
Crass, American, small-time grifter Freddie (Steve Martin) goes up against suave, British, big-time con man Lawrence (Michael Caine) on the French Riviera, in a battle to see who can scam the most money out of American heiress Glenne Headly in the funniest con man movie ever made.

HOUSE OF GAMES (1987) dir. David Mamet
Psychiatrist Margaret Ford (Lindsay Crouse) gets lured into the seedy under-world of grifters and con men when she learns that one of her patients owes Mike (Joe Mantegna) $25,000. Soon she's embroiled in a scam that has more twists and turns than Hampton Court maze.

CATCH ME IF YOU CAN (2002) dir. Steven Spielberg
Based on the true story of Frank Abagnale Jr., who—before his 19th birth-day—successfully cashed $2.5 million in dud checks around the world, while impersonating a Pan Am pilot, doctor, and legal prosecutor in the 1960s, before eventually becoming a fraud expert for the FBI.

21 (2008) dir. Robert Luketic
Inspired by the true story of group of MIT students who went to Atlantic City with a blackjack card counting system and made a fortune. In the film the team go to Las Vegas instead. While card counting isn't illegal per se, it's seri-ously frowned on by casinos, who have the right to ban suspected counters.

DIAMOND GEEZERS

O N NOVEMBER 7, 2000, AT 9:30AM, five men attempted to pull off the most audacious robbery of all time, stealing diamonds and jewels worth well over £203 million ($306 million) from the DeBeers exhibition at the Millennium Dome in London.

The plan was for Lee Wenham, Raymond Betson, William Cockram, Terry Millman, Aldo Ciarrocchi, Robert Adams, and Kevin Meredith to ram-raid the exhibit with a JCB digger, smash the cases with a nail gun and sledgehammer, and escape down the river Thames in a speedboat.

Dressed in body armor and gas masks the gang set off smoke bombs, and everything went smoothly for the first minute, until they were suddenly surrounded by over 200 police officers, 40 of them armed.

Unfortunately, the gang had been under Metropolitan Police surveillance for six months, after their two failed security van armed robberies. The police observed the gang casing the Dome, buying the speedboat, and had even managed to pin down the most likely days for the raid, based on the tide times. The police replaced the diamonds with fakes and the Dome staff with undercover officers, and allowed the gang to get into the vault " . . . where they were effectively imprisoned," the head of "Operation Magician," Detective Superintendent Jon Shatford, explained. The gang believed they were very close to succeeding, "I was 12 inches from pay day," Robert Adams revealed, "It would have been a blinding Christmas."

The gang members received between 5–18 years each for a variety of offences, including conspiring to rob. As Shatford stated, "Had it not been for the police they would have committed the largest robbery ever to take place anywhere in the world."

ACRONYMS: X, Y AND Z

X OR XTC: The drug MDMA (3,4-methylenedioxy-N-methamphetamine) also known as Ecstasy.

YOT: Youth Offending Team. UK agency that runs community services and reparation plans, and attempts to prevent youth recidivism and incarceration.

Z: Unfortunately we couldn't find a crime-related acronym beginning with Z, apart from ZPD, the Zanesville Police Department in Ohio. But that felt like cheating.

GARY RIDGWAY (1949-)

THROUGHOUT THE 1980S AND 1990S, Ridgway strangled numerous female victims in the Washington state area. The first five victims were found in the Green River and the press dubbed him "The Green River Killer." He had a love/hate relationship with prostitutes and many of his victims were escorts, because they were "easy to pick up" and he "hated most of them." The self-confessed "career" serial killer was also a necrophiliac, returning to his victims' corpses to have intercourse with them. Despite being interviewed as a potential suspect as far back as 1983, it wasn't until November 30, 2001, that enough DNA evidence was gathered to confirm he was the killer and he was arrested. To avoid the death penalty, Ridgway confessed to 48 unsolved murders, of which 42 were on the police's list of probable Green River Killer victims. He confessed to at least 71 murders, but the final total is believed to be more than 90. Convicted and sentenced to life imprisonment without parole, he remains incarcerated in Washington State Penitentiary.

INDEX

acronyms....9, 13, 16, 21, 24, 30, 34, 38, 41, 45, 51–52, 55, 59, 63, 65, ...68, 71, 75–76, 80, 85, 89, 92
Adams, John Bodkin..............61
Adams, Robert..............92
Agar, Edward..............6
Alcatraz..............76
animal hangings..............29

Badlands..............17, 75
Baldayev, Danzig..............67
Bananas, Joe..............54
Beane, Alexander..............82
beheading..............89
Benefit of Clergy..............20
Berkowitz, David..............50
Black, Antony..............74
The Black Museum..............78
Black, Robert..............33
Bloods..............59
Bonnot Gang..............43
Boston Strangler..............77
Boswell, James..............25, 55
Brady, Ian..............66
Brady, Patrick..............29
Brighton Trunk Murders..............12
Brink's-MAT robbery..............74
Broadmoor Asylum..............18
Buckley, William F...............19
Bundy, Ted..............13, 87
Buono, Angelo Jnr...............28
Buster..............75

Camorra..............9, 64
Camus, Albert..............35
cannibalism..............58, 82
capital punishment..............88–89
Capone, Al..............37, 76
Catch Me If You Can..............91
Chanal, Pierre..............47

Chapman's Protocol..............88
Charles, Robert..............85
Chessman, Caryl Whittier..............69
Clinch, Tom..............81
cocaine..............9, 60
Cohen, Stanley..............86
Conan Doyle, Arthur..............14, 78
confidence tricks..............13, 16, 25, 76, ...84, 91
Cornell, George..............15
Cosa Nostra..............19, 41
Costello, Frank..............83
costermongers..............65
Cotton, Mary Ann..............52
Crips..............59
crossroad burials..............24
cutpurses..............46

dactyloscopy..............14
DeBeers..............78, 92
Desalvo, Alberto..............77
Die Hard..............73
Dieudonné, Eugène..............43
Dirty Rotten Scoundrels..............91
DNA profiling..............34
Dostoyevsky, Fyodor..............60

Eastern State Penitentiary..............30
electric chairs..............88
Escobar, Pablo..............74
Evans, E.P...............29

fingerprints..............14
firing squads..............89
The First Great Train Robbery..............6
Fish, Hamilton..............58
Frost, Robert..............56
Garrotters Act..............86
gas chambers..............88
Gates, Daryl..............41

The Godfather 83, 86
Goldman, Emma 38
Gomorrah 64
Great Gold Robbery 6
The Grifters 91
Gulag 70

Hanging Mondays 35
hangings 35, 88
Hanratty, James 34
The Hatchet Man 46
Henry, Portrait of a Serial Killer
....75
highwaymen 55
Hindley, Myra 66
Hip Sings Tong 46
Horsemonger Lane Prison 21
House of Games 16, 91
hulks 15
Human Fly 37

Iceman 52

Jeffreys, Alec 34
Johnson, Samuel 25
Jonson, Ben 20

Kelly, Ned 10
Kray brothers 15
Kroll, Joachim 8
Kulinski, Richard 52

Landru, Henri D. 23
lethal injections 88
Ley, Thomas John 18
Liberti, Nello 64
Lucheni, Luigi 27
Lustig, Victor 76

McAvoy, Micky 74
Mafia 9, 19, 41, 50, 52, 64,
....68, 83, 86

Malcolm X 20
Man With 1000 Faces 38
Mancini, Tony 12
Manning, Maria and Frederick ...21
Manuel, Peter 36
Mayer, Johann 14
Mayhew, Henry 65
Mesrine, Jacques 38
Millennium Dome diamond
.... robbery 78, 92
Mock Duck 46
Mohocks 10
Mona Lisa robbery 25
moral panics 86
Morton, Jelly Roll 85
movies 6, 16, 46, 64, 73, 75, 83,
....87, 91
Muller, Franz 39
murder types 79

Nash, Ogden 82
Natural Born Killers 17
'Ndrangheta 9, 64
Neck Verse 20
Newgate Calendar 42, 57, 82
Newgate Prison 11, 22, 25, 35,
..............................39, 42, 51, 55
Noble, John 70
Noye, Kenneth 74

O'Brien, Jack 55
Old Bill 56
Omertà 54
On Leong Tong 46
Operation Magician 92
opium 46, 63
Orwell, George 56

Peel, Sir Robert 26
Petiot, Marcel 62
pickpockets 70
Pierrepoint, Albert 11

Pitchfork, Colin 34
poisons 63
police 10, 26, 56, 65
pressings 22
Prisoners' Property Act 78
prisons 11, 15, 30, 42
Propaganda of the Dead 27
Puente, Dorothea 72

Quick, Thomas 53

Rann, John 55
Ratcliff Highway Murders 40
Red Light Bandit 69
Ridgway, Gary 93
Riina, Totò 19, 86
10 Rillington Place 75
Robson, Brian 74
Rocancourt, Christophe 13
Rope 75

safe cracking 73
Salem witch trials 22
Santé Prison 38
Saviano, Roberto 24, 64
Schultz, Dutch 26
Scott, Peter 37
Search Bloc 74
Separate System 30
Shark Arm Murders 29
Shelton, "Stack" Lee 57
Sheppard, Jack 42
Siebert, Daniel Lee 90
Silence of the Lambs 87
Sixteen String Jack 55
slang 7, 31-32, 48–49, 84
Smith, Jim 29
Smith, Noel 67, 81
smuggling 9, 25, 60
Solzhenitsyn, Alexander 70
"Son of Sam" laws 50
Stalin, Josef 70

Starkweather, Charles 17, 75
The Sting 91
suicides 24
Sunday Morning Slasher 44
Swift, Jonathan 81

tattoos 67
Taxi Wars 54
thief-takers 51
Thompson, William 16
Tongs 46
Tyburn 25, 35, 42, 51, 55

United Nations Office on Drugs
and Crime 73, 89

Valachi, Joe 41
Valfierno, Eduardo de 25

Washington, Raymond 59
Washington State Penitentiary ... 93
Watts, Coral Eugene 44
Welles, Orson 78
Wild, Jonathan 51
Williams, John 40
Williams, Stanley 59

Yakuza 68
Yamaguchi-gumi 68

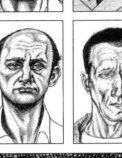